# The Live Pain Free® Cookbook

## 40 Simple Recipes to Eliminate Pain and Promote Healing

BY JESSE CANNONE CFT, CPRS, MFT WITH TIFFANY HARELIK, MA

# *The* Live Pain Free® COOKBOOK

## 40 Simple Recipes to Eliminate Pain and Promote Healing

BY JESSE CANNONE CFT, CPRS, MFT WITH TIFFANY HARELIK, MA

ISBN: 978-0-692-77084-9

Published by: Disk.com

Printed in the United States of America

# TABLE OF CONTENTS

# GRACE

FOREWORD BY TIFFANY HARELIK

Many generations of various cultural and spiritual backgrounds say grace before they eat a meal. But religious preferences aside, let us think about saying grace as an experiment. What if the simple act of being thankful for the food you are about to eat sends a message to the food that programs the food in such a way its very constituency is altered to help your body? I know this may sound ridiculous to some, but it is only ridiculous if it fails to work, right? So if saying grace before eating is not a regular part of your day, consider trying it as an experiment. All you have to do is get quiet, get thankful, and think positive, healing thoughts.

My experiment began when I met Dr. Masaru Emoto in Austin, Texas where he was giving a reading from his book, *The Hidden Messages in Water*. He had scientifically observed water after "showing" the water pictures and words, playing music to water and praying over the water. He used distilled water prepared to the same exacting standards as for hospital use. Every time he used positive words, beautiful images, pretty music and positive prayers, the water molecules transformed to a beautiful configuration. When he used negative words, harsh images, disturbing music and mean prayers, the water molecules became disfigured. His studies illustrated how sound and image frequencies alter water crystals in positive and negative ways.

After listening to him talk and reading his books, I decided to incorporate the science of positive thinking into my own life. In the morning, I write a word that I would like to infuse into my day on a small piece of paper and tape it to my water filter. The water filter is clear, so the water can 'see' the word and pick up the vibrational pattern. The word changes according to what type of vibrational medicine I want each day: joy, calm, peace, balance, wild, free, happy, abundance, health, service, fulfilled, etc. When I drink the water infused with whichever word I have selected, it subtly changes the frequency of my vibration accordingly.

Recent studies suggest Dr. Emoto's work *applies to food, too*. So doesn't it make sense to do everything possible to give yourself the best chance at overcoming pain and moving into optimal health? I am not telling you what to believe or what to say. I simply want you to think about it and figure out what works for you.

Think: what is your problem and what do you want this food to do for you? Give thanks out loud toward the water and food to help your body purify and nourish itself.

Do you know the saying that our lives are run by either memories or inspirations? You can use the wisdom of this advice and apply it toward health and eating. Consider the environment you are in while you are eating: who are you around, what kind of background music or television show is playing, how are you feeling? Let go of the memories of the day or the past, let go of any tensions and negativities, and try using a few inspirational words before each meal as part of this experiment.

I suggest that when you are joyful while cooking, this energy is transferred to the food and water, transforming the very molecules that you are about to eat. Once ingested, the frequency, or tone of those molecules will have a positive vibrational effect on your system and all those who you are cooking for and serving.

– Tiffany Harelik

# WHY YOU SHOULD READ THIS BOOK

## INTRODUCTION BY JESSE CANNONE, CFT, CPRS, MFT

If you are reading this book, you are probably in pain.

At one point or another every one of us experiences some type of pain. While pain is inevitable, it must be perceived as temporary.

It's the misconception of pain as "permanent" that leads to endless suffering. In other words, how you accept, respond to, adapt to and move through pain directly affects your ability to heal and finally end the pain.

We wrote this book to help you get out of pain by changing your perception of pain and suffering and providing specific strategies to beat chronic pain once and for all. It it you'll discover the nature of pain, including how your body's inflammatory response keeps you in pain and the role nutrition plays in getting you out of pain.

My name is Jesse Cannone. I am not a doctor nor do I hold any medical degrees, but as an author, fitness trainer and post-rehabilitation specialist, I've helped hundreds of thousands of people get out of pain without pharmaceutical drugs or surgery over the past 15 years.

As an advocate of cutting-edge alternative health ideas and curator of The Complete Healing Formula™, I have made it my life's work to help others reclaim their health through easy-to-follow methods such as those you'll find in this book.

While we explain The Complete Healing Formula™ in more detail in the first chapter of this book, it comes down to one core concept: balance. It may sound foreign at first, but **balance is the key to getting out of pain.**

We will talk about balance in the context of the four pillars supporting The Complete Healing Formula™: physical health, nutritional health, mental health and spiritual health.

We will discuss how any excess, deficiency or stagnation in these four areas creates imbalances in your system and how that results in pain.

Most importantly, by reading this book you will learn scientifically sound concepts you can apply starting immediately to relieve pain and get back on the road to health.

## Why Focus On Nutrition?

Balance in all four areas of The Complete Healing Formula™ is required for optimal health.

Physical imbalances likely play the most common role in creating pain. Yet even after addressing those physical imbalances, nutritional imbalances can keep you stuck in pain for life by contributing to the now ongoing inflammation-pain cycle.

The reason is simple: In our modern, industrialized society, our diet no longer supports healing and optimal health.

Cleveland dentist, Weston A. Price (1870-1948), travelled the world to study isolated, more primitive people groups to discover why they had perfect teeth and strong, healthy bodies. He discovered—especially as these groups left traditional diets to adopt modern dietary habits—that nutritional deficiencies introduce disease, pain and early death.

Our current diet, which increasingly consists of inflammatory processed foods and sugars largely void of whole food-sourced nutritional value, has left us susceptible to the ravages of chronic inflammation throughout our bodies—the underlying root cause of most disease and chronic pain today.

The good news is you can reverse this inflammatory trend through adjustments in your own diet to stop pain in its tracks. You don't have to embrace an entirely primitive hunter-gatherer diet to benefit. And you don't have to give up your favorite foods for good.

Instead, we'll show you how to identify your unique nutritional imbalances and take simple, corrective steps to tilt the balance back toward center. This action alone can dramatically reduce or completely end pain... despite any failed efforts you may have made in the past.

My co-author Tiffany's background illustrates this point well.

## Nutritional Balance: Your Key to Complete Recovery

Following a horrendous car accident at age 14 which fractured her spine and left her confined to bed for an entire summer, Tiffany suffered with significant back pain throughout the rest of her teens and 20s.

While the traumatic injuries created the initial pain, her muscles also overworked to compensate and protect the injury. The injury pinched her nerves and her tweaked back muscles worked overtime to compensate and protect her injured pulled spine, pulling it out of alignment, creating both nerve and tissue pain.

As a young woman, Tiffany worked in a chiropractic office, got frequent massages, obtained a Masters in Health Psychology and used essential oils. She stayed physically active, ate well and did everything she knew to do to improve her health, but pain still struck on occasion.

Tiffany told me how the pain became so unbearable it felt like she was having a heart attack during more stressful times. This is an example of how mental (emotional) imbalances like anxiety and pain can cause physical pain. Yet anxiety and pain were such a part of her life that it felt 'normal' whenever it occurred.

Tiffany continued to seek temporary relief with chiropractic appointments, acupuncture, massage and painkillers when the pain would flare up.

But it wasn't until she addressed inflammation from a dietary perspective, allowing her body to heal itself from the inside out, that she began to experience lasting relief. For Tiffany, those dietary changes meant eating more meats, vegetables and proteins and removing or reducing alcohol, wheat, dairy and excess sugars.

It was during a recent serendipitous encounter with Tiffany at a local hair salon where we both had appointments that I learned of our mutual interest in health and wellness, her success beating pain through dietary changes and her professional background in cookbooks.

Soon after, I enlisted Tiffany's help to share our combined knowledge of how to correct nutritional imbalances along with numerous favorite recipes you can use as-is or adapt with your favorite inflammation- and pain-relieving ingredients to create the book you now hold in your hands.

To my knowledge there has never been another book which so capably empowers you to eliminate pain and promote healing by addressing nutritional imbalances as this one. So read this book, mark the pages that speak to you most strongly and experiment with the recipes. Then most importantly, commit to fully enjoying a pain-free life once again.

Remember, life isn't about feeling better. It's about feeling your best.

# How to Use This Book

## What This Book Is Not

Before you dive into the main chapters, let me also take a moment to tell you what this book is *not*.

- This is not a weight loss book, although being overweight is a state of imbalance that can cause countless health problems. We will address this issue through the lens of excess and deficiency in diet and nutrition, but this book is not geared toward a weight loss strategy.

- This book is not a book about specific or targeted diets. Although we believe some fad diets offer a creative approach to restoring balance when followed properly, this book is not about fad dieting systems.

- This book is not partial to a particular cooking style, cooking heritage or cultural persuasion. The recipes within contain simple, cross-cultural ingredients most people can find at local grocery stores or order online.

- This is not a gluten-free cookbook. While we make every effort to minimize gluten intake, this is not a gluten-free specialty book.

- This is not a vegan vs. meat eaters cookbook. We respect differing points of view on eating meat. This book supports both omnivorous and vegetarian eating.

- This is not a blood-type diet book. We offer information on how you can utilize blood tests to help you understand where you may have nutritional imbalances, but this book is not geared toward diets for specific blood types.

- This book is not geared toward one spiritual path. We believe an individual's spirituality is one of the four crucial components of healing and optimal health, but we do not align with any particular sect or denomination.

## Who This Book Is For

This book is for anyone experiencing pain. Whether caused by a specific injury or due to a chronic disease or condition, we want you to understand that at its simplest, pain is a result of an inflammatory condition. Pain is a messenger for change. It's a call for action. It's your body asking you to address some imbalances. You do not have to live in pain nor learn how to manage it forever with medications. Pain can be your wake up call. You can learn how to work through it with the techniques and recipes we'll share in this book.

## Take a Personal Pain Inventory

Once you take into consideration the factors surrounding your pain and pain patterns, you can determine your imbalances and map out sustainable solutions. It might help you to take an inventory that includes the below items. From there, you have a base of knowledge to use in mapping out your personal plan for healing and optimal health.

- Your family medical history
- Personal eating patterns
- Personal exercise patterns
- Mental health
- Spiritual health
- Type of condition
- Severity of the condition
- Length of time you have had the condition
- What stage of healing you are currently in
- Your age
- Your body's metabolism

Here are some guidelines and basic steps to follow in working with this book:

1. **The advice in this book is not based on your diagnosis, severity of symptoms or even the location of your pain,** thus you will not find specific action steps or recipes for any one condition. The effectiveness of our nutritional approach is based on addressing the imbalances of nutrients in your diet.

   Your primary objective should be to work toward a more balanced approach to food, drinks and supplements in order to allow your body to heal itself *regardless* of the diagnosis or the symptoms you are feeling.

   **IMPORTANT:** You don't need to fix, change or cure your diagnosis to be pain free. Focus your energy on those things you control, like the way you think about what you are eating today and what you plan to eat in the future. This will allow your body to heal itself to the maximum extent that it can.

2. **Start slow and go slow**. Stay within your tolerance, making any dietary changes in moderation so they are easily incorporated. Making multiple drastic changes in your diet may help you return to a neutral state, but if those changes are unsustainable for you they won't be the best approach for long-term change and balanced nutrition. In fact, if you are far out of balance, eating super foods and highly nutritional foods may produce some initial discomfort in your system. Bear in mind, everyone is in a different stage of healing. You may need to incorporate some of the strategies in this book slower than another person who may be farther along in their healing process.

3. **Stick to your plan**. I will give you some fundamental ideas to incorporate into your daily life, but it is up to you to implement what I teach. The length of time it takes for you to get relief from pain depends largely on how well you stick to

your plan. Expect good days and bad days. Don't quit if you don't see results as quickly as you would like. Stay the course.

4. **There is no required order to the recipes** you should incorporate first or on any given day. What you eat and how much you eat should all be done with a balanced approach.

5. **Drink plenty of water** throughout the day to stay hydrated and help flush toxins from your bloodstream.

## KEY POINTS:

- We encourage you to open your eyes to new concepts: be willing to take a chance on changing habits and patterns you've followed for decades. That type of change is the only way you'll experience significant improvement.

- If you're reading this book and you're in pain, your body is stuck. Your body tries to heal itself every second of every minute, but your body can't work past some situations on its own. You'll need to give it a helping hand when an excess or deficiency creates an imbalance that prevents you from moving beyond your current stage of healing.

- The information in this book will educate you and protect you from much of the misinformation floating around on the internet. Our principles will enable you to choose food and nutrition in a way that creates balance for your body and gives your body the best opportunity to heal itself.

- You will learn that most of our health conditions and challenges, including pain, derive from a state of imbalance. Imbalances occur when we have an excess or deficiency in nutrition, thought patterns or even our spiritual path.

We invite you to open your mind to the idea of experimenting with what we know works. If you can shift your thoughts, patterns and habits in the small arena of nutrition and meal planning with the help of the information in this book, you will feel better over time... and not just feel better, but maximize your life to its full potential.

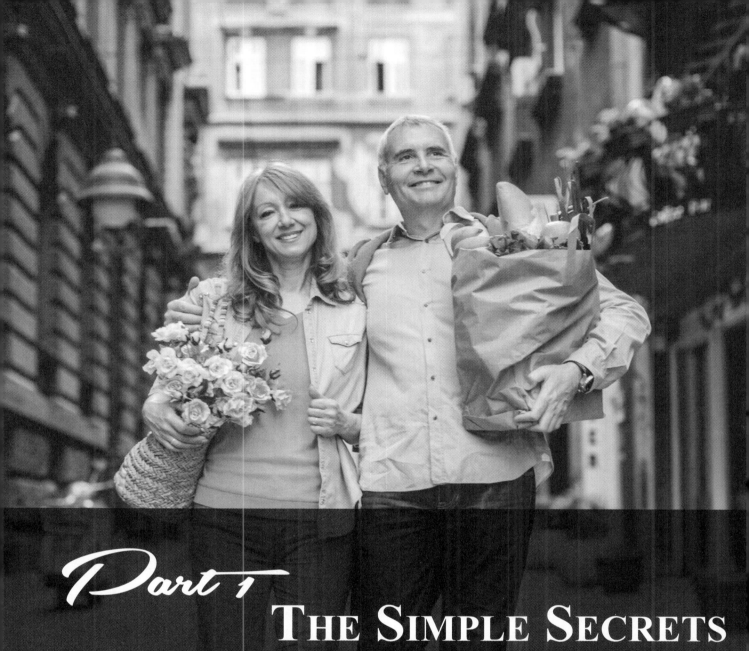

# Part 1
## THE SIMPLE SECRETS OF LIVING PAIN FREE

# Introducing
# the Complete Healing Formula™

### The Complete Healing Formula™

The concept behind The Complete Healing Formula™ is not new information. It is a compilation of ancient information presented in a new way that makes it easy to understand and utilize to treat pain.

I have taught hundreds of thousands of people all over the world this approach to pain relief. It can work for you, too.

The Complete Healing Formula™ states this: Everything matters in the concept of healing.

### Balance and Harmony

There are four main pillars of health we include: physical, nutritional, mental and spiritual. The Complete Healing Formula™ is based on balancing and harmonizing those four main pillars of health. If you address balance in all of those areas, there is no way you can't feel better.

The body is constantly trying to heal itself. Yet if we are out of balance in any of these four areas (physical, nutritional, mental or spiritual), healing becomes impossible. This means that even if your physical and nutritional areas are in balance, but your thoughts, feelings and emotions are not balanced, you will never reach an optimal state of being and vice versa. Balance and harmony in all four pillars are required for maximum health.

Let's dive a little deeper into how each of these pillars affect your health:

## Physical

Our physical body includes muscles, bones, organs, nerves, tendons, ligaments, tissues and cartilage. Each group has a specific job to keep our body functioning.

While muscles make movement possible, consider also how they hold everything in place. They control the way your spine maintains it's shape, the angle of your pelvis, the tightness of your joints and so on.

## Muscle Imbalances

All muscles have a certain amount of strength and a certain amount of flexibility. When imbalanced, one set of muscles become overly strengthened and tight, overpowering their opposing set of muscles which become weaker and stretched out.

For example, if you sit all day you'll tend to have tight hip flexor muscles (the muscle in the front of the upper leg) and weak glutes (that would be your butt muscles) due to how your muscles are used–or not used–when maintaining a seated position.

This single muscle imbalance creates a cascade of problems leading to pain:

1. The muscle imbalance pulls your hips from a healthy, neutral position to a forward tipping position.

2. Your spine, which connects to your pelvis, creates an abnormal curvature to compensate for the tilt in your hips.

3. This spinal misalignment creates painful inflammation, muscle tension and spinal compression which can pinch nerves.

It's no surprise then muscles are one of the biggest causes of inflammation and two types of pain: tissue pain and nerve pain. Although the most common muscle imbalances we see are in the hips and pelvis, muscle imbalances can pull any area of your body out of alignment such as your pelvis, spine, knees, ankles, shoulders, etc.

When looking for holistic solutions to get out of pain, understand you may have to address both tissue pain and nerve pain for complete relief.

## Tissue Pain

Unequal strength in muscle groups is one common way tissue pain can manifest. In the muscle imbalance example above, your pelvis becomes unstable and tips forward. This results in friction, tension, inflammation and therefore pain. Strength and flexibility exercises as well as a low inflammatory diet can help put your body back in balance and harmony.

## Nerve Pain

Uneven force applied to your spine by muscle imbalances can cause spinal compression and contortion that pinch nerves, especially as they exit your spinal column, resulting in nerve pain. A herniated disc is one way such nerve pain can manifest. Surgery is often recommended by doctors to remove the object (your herniated disc) that is putting pressure on the nerve causing pain. A more holistic approach using The Complete

Healing Formula™ would be to address the underlying cause of the nerve pain–the muscle imbalance.

## Finding a More Holistic Approach

When searching for non-surgical relief from pain ultimately caused by muscle imbalances, many follow a similar pattern. We'd like to briefly examine some of the shortcomings of that approach to help you get well faster.

Let's say you have low back pain and start by visiting a physical therapist. Chances are they will give you the same cookie cutter exercise they give everyone with back pain and miss the opportunity to address a specific muscle imbalance.

As a next step, maybe you go to a chiropractor who explains to you that pressure from your spine is pinching nerves and causing pain. Chiropractic patients are often asked to return over and over. However, if the spinal misalignment you have is likely due primarily to muscle imbalances.

*Ask yourself, is the medical professional you're seeing treating your symptoms or the root cause of your condition?*

In either case, if you overlook the importance of balancing muscle groups, your chiropractic adjustments and physical therapy exercises may not hold. A manipulation or adjustment may provide temporary relief as you get the bones to go back into their proper place, but without helping the muscles adjust as well you may find yourself still in pain.

Please note we are not saying to avoid physical therapy or chiropractic. Our goal is to educate you so that you can get the best results possible. Corrective exercises and stretches that help resolve imbalances will only help your chiropractic adjustment hold or physical therapy exercises resolve your pain.

Ultimately our message is this: if you do not address the four pillars we suggest in The Complete Healing Formula™, you may be missing a critical piece of your pain puzzle.

## KEY POINTS:

- Muscle imbalances cause inflammation and pain.

- The key thing to remember about muscle imbalances is that we are always talking about two opposing muscle groups, where one has more strength than the other and is pulling your body into less than optimal positions creating unnecessary strain, inflammation and pressure.

- Remember to look at your body as a whole and not just zoom in to the problem area. You may have back pain due to an imbalance in the muscles around your ankles. But if you are only trying to treat back pain without looking at the whole body system, you may miss some very important clues.

- Muscle imbalances do not occur because you are weak. They occur because one area is overly strong or is used more than the other.

- Balanced muscles allow for harmony and proper movement and muscle mechanics.

## Nutrition

Nutrition is the second pillar of The Complete Healing Formula™. In addition to considering balance within our physical health, we must also look at balance within our nutrition to get a clear holistic picture.

What you eat plays a role in how well you heal and how much pain you feel. If you eat the same thing over and over and over again you will create imbalances within your diet. A balanced diet includes various sources of proteins, vegetables, fruits and fiber.

### Eat the rainbow.

One easy way to ensure you eat a variety of foods is to eat different colors of foods. At a basic level, each color on the spectrum provides different nutrients that assist with different functions.

Here are some ideas on how you can eat the rainbow:

- Red: beets, apples, strawberries, watermelon
- Orange: carrots, oranges, pumpkins, cantaloupe, sweet potatoes
- Yellow: bananas, squash, lemons
- Green: spinach, kale, celery, pears, cucumbers, artichokes
- Blue: blueberries
- Purple: eggplant, some carrots, some potatoes, blackberries
- White: garlic, onion, potatoes, cashews, macadamia nuts
- Brown: almonds, walnuts, brazil nuts

## Most of us aren't eating properly.

In general, we don't eat mindfully. As a result we tend to:

- Be minerally deficient
- Ingest chemicals
- Ingest preservatives
- Ingest toxins in our water
- Ingest hormones in meat & dairy

## Do what you can to clean up your diet.

- Filter your water
- Wash your fruits and vegetables with organic solutions
- Rinse your meat before cooking it
- Buy organic, unprocessed foods when possible
- Buy nitrate-free, free-range or responsibly raised meat when possible

## Cut out the primary offenders when you can.

- High fructose corn syrup
- Sugar
- Fried foods
- Wheat
- Dairy
- Gluten
- GMOs
- MSG
- Foods high in fat
- Partially hydrogenated soybean oil
- Anything processed or in a box

## If you're in pain and need to get out of inflammation, try incorporating these quick anti-inflammatory foods in your diet:

- **Turmeric:** buy it in bulk and remove the skin. Grate it like a carrot and add it fresh to any salad, tea or smoothie.

- **Beets:** bake at 400° F for about an hour or until desired tenderness. Once cooled, remove the skin. Slice into rounds and layer with orange slices for a simple two-ingredient beet salad.

- **Berries:** try a berry salad with raspberries, blueberries and blackberries.

- **Ginger:** chop in large chunks and boil in water to make a tea. Add honey and lemon to taste.

- **Garlic and onions:** these inflammation-fighting foods are a great flavor combination to add to any roasted vegetable dish such as broccoli or potatoes.

- **Cacao:** add some cacao to your coffee or smoothie.

- **Green tea:** drink this as an afternoon pick-me-up. Note: if you are using raw honey to sweeten this tea, you will be killing the beneficial properties of raw honey if you pour it into hot tea. Alternatively, wait until the tea has cooled to add honey, or try xylitol or lemon in hot tea instead.

## KEY POINTS:

- Imbalances in your food and diet reduce your body's ability to heal quickly on it's own. If your body has to spend energy to compensate for an imbalance in the fuel you are giving it, your body will operate in a less than optimal state. It is imperative to eat a balanced diet with proper nutrition to allow your body to enter its healing mode.

- You might be getting full when you eat, but that does not mean you are getting quality nutrients.

- When you are in pain and stressed, your body requires a higher caloric intake and more nutrients.

- A major part of the pain puzzle is inflammation. The more you can reduce inflammation through diet, the better. Sometimes that alone is enough for you to get pain relief.

## Mental Health

Mental health is the third pillar of The Complete Healing Formula™. But we're not talking about mental disorders. Instead, we're referring to how your mindset, emotions and beliefs affect your overall health. And as a result, why you must strive for balance in your mental state to reduce pain and live at an optimal state of health and well-being.

Consider this: our thoughts, feelings and emotions are all part of our mental health. And we all have unresolved emotional issues and we all handle stress and negative emotions in different ways. But if we remain in a constant state of negative thoughts and emotions, we will never be able to get to a healing state.

Mental stress prompts your body to alter hormonal flow which over prolonged periods overworks your adrenal glands and wreaks havoc in your body. Another physical response to these negative emotions and stress is muscle tension tightness which directly influences tissue pain and nerve pain.

In addition to your mind's ability to directly create conditions ripe for pain, it also plays a role in our cooking and eating habits. If you have a mindset that preparing a healthy dish of food is difficult, even if you acknowledge the health benefits, you are unlikely to buy the needed ingredients and take the time to learn how to make it. Thus, your mindset prevents you from making a potentially very positive change in your cooking and eating habits.

In order to overcome this cognitive dissonance, you will need to retrain your mind. There are several emotional release techniques you can try at home including EFT and

The Sedona method. A quick online search will offer you unlimited videos and training techniques. You can also retrain your mind with simple self-coaching mantras that spiral your thinking up such as:

1. I acknowledge I am not very open to learning new cooking techniques.

2. I acknowledge I value my health.

3. I am willing to learn new things to get out of pain.

4. I am willing to make time to try a new way of cooking this week.

5. I will find a way to make this new approach more enjoyable either by inviting a friend to either teach me how or learn to make this new food together.

## Strategies for balancing mental health:

- Schedule a mental health day.

- Spend 30 minutes to an hour outside every day.

- Spend 10 minutes with your bare feet in the dirt, grounding every day.

- Do some breath work or meditate in the morning to clear your mind and prepare for the day.

- Set daily intentions and write notes to put on your mirror. This will keep your intentions and affirmations in front of you and top of mind.

- Give your mind breaks throughout the day.

- Seek professional help with counselors and healers as needed.

- Make a gratitude list each night before you go to bed. Literally count your blessings so they are in your thoughts as you go to sleep.

- Notice your negative thoughts (impatience, unkindness, jealousy, anger, etc.) and rate them on a scale from one to ten. One means you are experiencing the negative thinking less and ten meaning you are experiencing the negative thinking at maximum. Now notice the opposite of that negative thought and rate that as well. For example, if you are at an 8 on the impatience scale, you only have 2 left for patience. Ask yourself how willing you are to let go of the negative thoughts and slide toward more positive thoughts. Keep a thorough thought journal for at least a week to notice your progress.

**KEY POINTS:**
- Your mental health affects your physical health.
- Stress and negative emotions can cause muscle constriction which can create painful muscle tension, pinch or stress nerves, and create any number of harmful chemical / hormonal imbalances.
- Mental health is an important pillar in The Complete Healing Formula™.

## Spirituality

You may have heard Pierre Teilhard de Chardin's quote: "We are not human beings having a spiritual experience; we are spiritual beings having a human experience." This logic resonates with The Complete Healing Formula™ in that mind and body health are inseparable. In addition to Chardin's quote, several major religions acknowledge our bodies are the houses of our spiritual selves and therefore worthy of care. To take care of your spirit, you have an opportunity to exercise faith in a higher power. In a more practical sense: prayer and meditation when done in co-creation with your higher power can be catalysts to healing.

Spiritual health is unique to each person. To help you define your spiritual health, try taking an inventory of various spiritual qualities and their opposites. Rate yourself on each of the qualities on a scale from 1 to 10. This information will help you see how much room you have for growth in each quality. Consider taking inventory on a daily basis to gather information. Then, at the end of the week, look for patterns in your data. Did you spend a majority of your days being impatient or intolerant of certain people, places or things?

Here are a few spiritual qualities and their opposites you can use in your inventory:

- Patience (Impatience)
- Tolerance (Intolerance)
- Compassion (Indifference)
- Humility (Pride)
- Trust/Faith (Fear)
- Sympathy (Resentment)
- Love (Hate)

Spiritual health is not a race and there is nothing to win or gain other than internal peace. With the information you gather in your inventory, you can begin to note areas you would like to improve. Your attention to these areas will increase, prompting you to make a few changes. If you notice you have been intolerant, you will be more likely to sense yourself becoming intolerant sooner and have opportunity to self-correct earlier the next time. If you notice your impatience has been at a 9 all week, that means you have only been at a 1 on patience. The next time you feel impatience rising, see how willing you are to take it from a 9 to an 8, and so on.

We have extracted some quotes from various texts and philosophic perspectives to illustrate the common thread: it is imperative to take care of your body by also taking care of your spiritual health through prayer, meditation and faith in a higher power.

*"That deeply emotional conviction of the presence of a superior reasoning power, which is revealed in the incomprehensible universe, forms my idea of God."* ALBERT EINSTEIN

*"Do you not know that your bodies are temples of the Holy Spirit, who is in you, whom you have received from God? You are not your own; you were bought at a price. Therefore honor God with your bodies."* 1 CORINTHIANS 6:19-20 NEW INTERNATIONAL VERSION (NIV)

*"Learn to get in touch with the silence within yourself and know that everything in this life has a purpose. There are no mistakes, no coincidences. All events are blessings given to us to learn from."* ELIZABETH KÜBLER-ROSS

*"Imagine that every person in the world is enlightened but you. They are all your teachers, each doing just the right things to help you learn perfect patience, perfect wisdom, perfect compassion."* BUDDHA

*"Qualities like love and compassion are not just abstract virtues that are the property of saints and adepts. Anyone can develop these qualities in themselves by doing spiritual practices. As the Buddha said, Come and see."* JOANNA MACY

*"Big-heartedness is the most essential virtue on the spiritual journey."* MATTHEW FOX

*"Each one has to find his peace from within. And peace to be real must be unaffected by outside circumstances."* MAHATMA GANDHI

*"Prayer at its highest is a two-way conversation–and for me the most important part is listening to God's replies."* FRANK C. LAUBACH

*"Empty yourself of everything. Let the mind rest at peace. The ten thousand things rise and fall while the Self watches their return. They grow and flourish and then return to the source. Returning to the source is stillness, which is the way of nature."* LAO TZU

*"We're fields of energy in an infinite energy field."* E.E. CUMMINGS

It is of utmost importance to make sure your spiritual life is balanced to effect positive change on the way your body feels. It's ok if you do not affiliate with a specific religion or spiritual practice, but we do not want you to underestimate the value of a spiritual practice in the bigger picture of your overall health and wellness. At the most basic level: when the mind is not well, that has an effect on the body. Your spiritual nature and health are as critical to your physical performance as proper eating and muscle rebalancing.

The point of this section is not to convince you to adhere to a stringent set of spiritual practices to transform your pain. Rather, we invite you to connect with your inner divine nature in whatever ways you have available in your toolkit. The simple spiritual practices below will help put you in a better balanced state of mind. And again, balancing the four pillars of The Complete Healing Formula™ is our map to remove pain and live in optimal health.

**Easy practices to incorporate:**

- Say "thank you" more often
- Say "I'm sorry" if you need to
- Say "you're welcome" with gratitude
- Be of service to others

- Say "I love you" authentically Spend regular time each day in meditation and prayer
- Take your spiritual qualities inventory (see above)

**KEY POINTS:**

- Spiritual health is one of the four pillars of The Complete Healing Formula™.

- Utilize whatever spiritual practices you enjoy to create calmness, peace, harmony, tranquility and balance in your mind and heart.

- Read books, attend spiritual gatherings and learn more about spirituality so you can find and participate in a supportive and like-minded community.

## Why Everything Matters with The Complete Healing Formula™

Treating only one particular area for one particular source of pain is unlikely to eliminate all chronic pain. That's why The Complete Healing Formula™ helps you cover all the bases to balance your system holistically and set yourself up for optimal wellness.

Remember, health care professionals rarely tell you this because most treat only one symptom in one area (physical, nutrition, mind or spirit).

We have discussed treating imbalances within physical, nutritional, mental and spiritual perspectives at a basic level of The Complete Healing Formula™. The next step is to understand where these imbalances come from and how we can address each one.

## Excess, Deficiency and Stagnation

We derive our philosophy from an ancient Asian perspective that says excesses and deficiencies lead to stagnation. Stagnation is important, because that is the phase where pain comes into play.

If you are healthy and feeling well with adequate nutrition and movement, you are not in a state of stagnation. But if you are experiencing excesses or deficiencies in any of the four areas of The Complete Healing Formula™, these imbalances lead to stagnation and eventually pain if not addressed.

### The difference between excess and deficiency.

Too much of one thing (excess) can lead to not enough (deficiency) of the other. For example, if we have excessive spending habits (excess), and not enough income (deficiency), these circumstances will lead to a painful stagnation such as debt.

This excess/deficiency principle can be applied to all four areas of The Complete Healing Formula™. Let's look at some specific examples:

### Physical Imbalance Example

Being overweight without enough movement causes an imbalance in health and therefore pain.

- Excess: Too much weight.
- Deficiency: Not enough movement.
- Stagnation: Stagnant weight and being overweight causes multiple health concerns including but not limited to joint pain.
- Action Plan: Reduce weight by reducing caloric intake while increasing physical activity. Establish goals that include meal plans, workouts and a daily recap/journal to mark progress.

### Nutritional Imbalance Example

Too much calcium with insufficient vitamin D3 to tell the body what to do with the calcium causes imbalances and stagnations.

- Excess: Too much calcium.
- Deficiency: Not enough vitamin D3.

- Stagnation: Urinary issues, constipation, bone spurs, etc.
- Action Plan: Monitor calcium and vitamin D3 levels through blood work and supplement accordingly. The body must do something with your calcium intake. If it doesn't have enough vitamin D3, the calcium stagnates within the body causing imbalances and health dilemmas.

## Mental Health Imbalance Example

Excessive stress and an inability to handle it causes an imbalance in stress-related hormones. This imbalance creates inflammation, which is a stagnation in recovery.

- Excess: Too much stress and negative thoughts/emotions.
- Deficiency: Insufficient rejuvenation and relaxation.
- Stagnation: Increased cortisol hormone level and exacerbated stress on the adrenal glands produces inflammation in the body, decreased blood flow and overall inability to heal.
- Action Plan: Review blood work to determine if you require nutritional supplements to counter adrenal stress and/or balance hormones. Calendar time for mental health best practices such as: listen to helpful podcasts on the topic that is causing your stress; talk with a friend or therapist; take a break from thinking about your stress (schedule a mental health day); learn about new coping mechanisms to handle your stress in a non-toxic way.

## Spiritual Imbalance Example

If you have an excess of negativity in the spiritual pillar, this will create a deficiency of the 'good things' in life which results in a stagnation and imbalance in your spiritual path.

- Excess: Increased negative traits such as greed, ambition, anger, lust, always wanting more and selfish cravings.
- Deficiency: Lack of positive traits such as gratitude, appreciation, compassion and approval of others.
- Stagnation: Happiness, love and peace elude you.
- Action Plan: Learn to forgive yourself and others, let go of never ending desires for more and give more instead (you may just find you get more in the end).

# Stages of Healing

The proper treatment or action plan depends on where you are on the spectrum of healing within the four pillars of The Complete Healing Formula™.

Consider where you are now in each of these four areas of health the ask yourself: Should you address mental stressors first? Should you address physical therapy at the same time you start a new nutritional plan? Should you focus on spiritual aspects of your life more?

**When something is not working, make a change. Take new action!**

Although it can take longer than we would like to get out of chronic pain at times, be conscious of your progress in healing your pain. At a certain point, if you are not improving, it's time to reevaluate your plan and how you're following it.

- Make a checklist. Even if you thought you have done everything, it's possible you neglected an area of The Complete Healing Formula™ your checklist will reveal. If you find yourself thinking, "I've done everything I can and nothing seems to work," remind yourself there are always other things you can try.

- Realize you may need to change your mindset to get results. Is cognitive dissonance affecting your treatment action plan? Cognitive dissonance is the state of having inconsistent thoughts, beliefs or attitudes relative to behavioral decisions and changes. For example, if you are told to do a specific stretch to return your muscles to a more balanced state but in the back of your mind believe stretching won't help you out of pain, your own mindset blocks your ability to heal. If you start your plan with an objection to doing the very thing that may help you get out of pain, it is less likely to work for you.

- Cognitive dissonances apply to food, too. For example, if someone tells you to eat a certain food to feel better, and you eat it but do not feel better immediately, you may develop a belief that 'this food won't work to get me out of pain' before you have given the new diet enough time to work.

- To take effective action, you have to educate yourself on why a plan will work so you can make the change without objecting to the change or potential solution.

- Keep asking yourself questions: Will this work for me? Is this the most appropriate action for me? In time, you will know what works–and what doesn't–for you and your pain-free program.

**Recovery Goals: Why Change?**

Recovery goals matter. Don't underestimate the power of goal setting and envisioning a life free from pain in your recovery. Below are some exercises that will help you establish your own recovery goals:

- Write goal sentences about why you want to make changes. Ultimately, you want to get out of pain, but why else do you want to get better? Let this why remind you what you want to do after you feel better and give you the impetus to accept change and break through any cognitive dissonance you may experience during your journey. Example: I want to get out of pain so that I can enjoy hiking with my daughter.

- Write goals for using this book. Example: I am going to try five new foods and three new ways to prepare breakfast.

- List your goals and categorize them from The Complete Healing Formula™ perspective: physical, nutritional, mental health or spiritual.

- Make a list of things you can identify in your life that are creating imbalances and then work toward balance. What are you doing too much of? What are you not doing enough of? Take a piece of paper and create three columns: excess, deficiency, stagnation. Fill in the columns with things you have too much of, not enough of and where you are stagnant. You'll find that one thing leads to another and you have plenty you can start to work on right away. It's a powerful exercise and an easy way to see what areas need the most attention.

## KEY POINTS:

- In life, our bodies strive for balance (homeostasis). There should be balance in all four areas. It's easy to get out of balance.

- Health problems typically result from a mix of imbalances. Rarely do they result from a single imbalance. Incorporate all areas of The Complete Healing Formula™ (physical, nutritional, mental health and spiritual) in your approach to get lasting pain relief.

- Write goals with a daily recap. What have you done to change stagnation today?

# The Complete Healing Formula™ and Nutrition

When it comes to addressing the root cause and symptoms of pain, everything matters. The Complete Healing Formula™ is a comprehensive, holistic approach to eliminating pain.

In the previous chapter we briefly reviewed the four primary areas of health within The Complete Healing Formula™: physical, nutritional, mental health and spirituality. Within these areas we look for excesses, deficiencies and stagnations. Restoring balance to all four areas improves health and ends pain.

## Dietary Balance

Ask yourself: is your diet balanced or imbalanced? If you are in pain, chances are your current diet plays a role. Eating more foods that fight pain-causing inflammation and less that are inflammatory addresses the most common dietary imbalance. However, other nutritional and dietary imbalances will likely need to be addressed for complete relief.

### Excess, deficiency and stagnation: more nutrition examples.

As we discussed in the last chapter, excesses and deficiencies in your diet play a role in creating pain-causing stagnation. Here are some more examples to help you further understand this concept as it relates to your diet.

### Example 1: Bulk and Fiber

In addition to keeping you regular, fiber helps carry toxic buildup out of your system. If you eat too much food (excess) without enough fiber (deficiency), you will have constipation (stagnation). Cheese, meat and other foods that tend to get stuck in your digestive tract are must be balanced with fiber-rich vegetables, nuts and beans.

### Example 2: Omega-6 Fatty Acid and Omega-3 Fatty Acid

We should all strive to do a better job of balancing omega 6-fatty acids with omega-3 fatty acids. While both are essential, we tend to eat too many omega-6 fatty acids in our western diet and not enough omega-3s. Many of the omega-6s we eat come from vegetable oils used to prepare processed foods, chips and popcorn while omega-3s are more prevalent in fish, walnuts and grass-fed beef.

If you ingest too many omega-6 fatty acids (excess) and not enough omega-3 fatty acids (deficiency) you condition your body in a way that promotes arthritis, osteoporosis, decreased brain function, inflammation and pain (stagnation).

## Avoid Dietary Sabotage Through Emotional Eating

Emotional eating and other unhealthy eating habits can sabotage healthy meal planning and your overall healing strategy. This is where the interplay of physical, nutritional, mental health and spiritual aspects of The Complete Healing Formula™ work against you unless you remain mindful of your eating patterns. Recognizing the signs and planning ahead can minimize the impact.

### Strategies to avoid emotional eating

When you think you are hungry, ask yourself:

- Am I actually thirsty as opposed to hungry?
    - Dehydration can sometimes have the same effect as feeling hungry. Drink a full glass of water before grabbing a bite to eat.
- Am I angry, lonely, tired or in an otherwise negative state of mind?
    - These feelings may be warning of low nutrition in which case you should take care of yourself and eat something healthy. Regular, appropriately-portioned meals and light, healthy snacks may prevent this. But if you notice you eat to self-soothe from one of these emotions, perhaps take a walk, do some yoga, perform some breathing exercises or some other calming activity instead of opening the refrigerator.
- Stock your pantry and fridge with healthy options.
    - If you are trying to break a habit of emotional eating or unhealthy eating, and you know you are going to walk over to the fridge, at least make sure it is stocked with healthy options that will nourish you rather than junk food.
- Is my state of mind taking me closer to or further away from my goal of living pain free?
    - Use some tools, statements or mantras to spiral your thoughts up and away from bad eating habits:

- "I'm aware this isn't the best choice for me and I'm willing to make a change."
- "I have a few options here and I'm going to choose the best one for me right now."
- "I'm working a plan to be more balanced with my dietary decisions and this food will be good for me."

## Basic Nutritional Requirements

Once meal planning becomes a habit, you can ensure you get the basic nutritional requirements in your diet. The food source guidelines below will help you incorporate a balance of minerals, vitamins and enzymes in every meal.

However, the recommended dietary allowance (RDA) is set for healthy individuals. If you are in pain, the normal RDA does not apply to you. You will most likely need a therapeutic dose of certain vitamins and nutrients if you are suffering from chronic pain, if you are older, or if you are engaged in increased athletic activity.

Since nutrient requirements change based on age, health and activity level, they also need to change if you are deficient or have excess in any area. Regular blood tests will help you monitor your minerals and vitamins and give you a baseline from which to decide which foods and supplements you should incorporate at a different level than the standard RDA.

Certain medications as well as caffeine and alcohol intake can reduce your body's ability to absorb vital nutrients and/or cause the nutrients to be expelled before they have a chance to enter your bloodstream. They can also inhibit enzymes from converting nutrients into nourishment for your body.

You may want to consider supplementation as part of your healthy eating strategy, especially if you know you are not eating in a balanced manner. If you are on medication for any reason, it is best to work with your primary doctor to establish a supplemental plan that is complementary to your overall health care regimen.

### Minerals

If you find yourself needing to supplement with minerals, choose a full spectrum trace mineral product sourced from the sea. Let's break down exactly what that means.

Full spectrum simply means including the broadest possible array of minerals and other elements your body requires for

**All food is NOT created equal.**

Our soils are depleted from nutrients, conventionally grown food may have harmful chemicals, etc. Be aware that storing food for extended periods or cooking at higher temperatures reduces nutritional value. Fresh foods provide the most nutrition while frozen foods preserve the most nutrition in storage.

good health. We know of at least 92 elements and nearly 2/3rds are vital to maintaining health–yet experts suggest as many as 90% of Americans are deficient in many of them, causing significant mineral imbalances.

Your body requires many minerals and other elements in only tiny, or trace, amounts. These are most readily found in sea-sourced supplements. However, be sure to choose a mineral supplement low in sodium that comes from healthy (not polluted or radioactive) waters.

Let's take a closer look at some key minerals we need for health and wellness:

**Calcium**
- Where you can find it: cabbage, kale, broccoli
- What it does for the body: promotes bone health
- Symptoms of excess: Without vitamin D3 to help bones absorb it, excess calcium settles in arteries and bones causing bone spurs, muscle pain, mood disorders, kidney stones
- Symptoms of deficiency: numbness and/or tingling in fingers, osteoporosis

**Chromium**
- Where you can find it: broccoli, whole grains (barley, oats), green beans
- What it does for the body: improves digestion, blood sugar and energy regulation
- Symptoms of excess: stomach/digestive problems
- Symptoms of deficiency: increased risk of glaucoma

**Folate**
- Where you can find it: dark leafy greens, asparagus, broccoli, citrus fruit
- What it does for the body: aids cell division and repair
- Symptoms of excess: There is no risk of getting too much folate from food sources. However, taking excessive amounts of folic acid from supplements rather than getting folate naturally from food may cause digestive issues, sleep problems and even various psychoses.
- Symptoms of deficiency: anemia

**Iron**
- Where you can find it: beef, chicken, oysters, clams, beans, spinach, lentils
- What it does for the body: carries oxygen to our lungs
- Symptoms of excess: iron poisoning, abdominal pain, bloody stool, dehydration
- Symptoms of deficiency: anemia, shortness of breath, brittle hair and nails, cold hands and feet

### Magnesium

- Where you can find it: dark leafy greens, nuts, seeds, fish
- What it does for the body: bone health, relaxes tight muscles, important electrolyte
- Symptoms of excess: irregular heartbeat, low blood pressure
- Symptoms of deficiency: sleeplessness, teeth issues, bone issues, muscle cramps

### Potassium

- Where you can find it: potatoes, beets, dark leafy greens, bananas
- What it does for the body: nerve, muscle and heart health
- Symptoms of excess: dehydration, internal bleeding, nausea, chest pain
- Symptoms of deficiency: tingling, numbness, nausea, constipation, abdominal cramping or bloating

### Selenium

- Where you can find it: Brazil nuts, mussels, octopus, tuna fish, sunflower seeds, beef, pork, lamb, chicken, turkey, mushrooms
  - What it does for the body: aids thyroid function
  - Symptoms of excess: bad breath, diarrhea, hair loss
  - Symptoms of deficiency: muscle and joint pain, brittle hair and nails, Hashimoto's disease in extreme cases

### Sodium

- Where you can find it: your salt shaker
- What it does for the body: controls fluid balances and assists with muscle/nerve health
- Symptoms of excess: high blood pressure, bloating, kidney strain, edema, swelling
- Symptoms of deficiency: hyponatremia, headaches, muscle spasms, nausea, seizures

### Zinc

- Where you can find it: cooked oysters, spinach, pumpkin seeds, nuts, cocoa, mushrooms
- What it does for the body: maintains a sense of smell, immune system health, builds proteins, triggers enzymes, creates DNA
- Symptoms of excess: nausea and vomiting, headaches, disrupts the ability to absorb copper and iron

## Iodized table salt or sea salt?

With small amounts of trace minerals and better flavor, sea salt is a better choice than iodized table salt. However, its high sodium content still makes it unsuitable as a supplement. Use it sparingly at the dinner table instead of iodized table salt, but not as a replacement for a full spectrum ionic trace mineral supplement which should include the additional iodine you need in addition to the small amount found in sea salt.

- Symptoms of deficiency: diarrhea, impotence, hair loss, impaired immune system function, stunted growth

## Vitamins: Eat the Alphabet

Vitamins and minerals both work in a cascade fashion, meaning one needs the next to perform a task which needs the next to perform a task and so on. If you want to use supplements for vitamins, choose 'whole food vitamin' supplements to ensure you get all the bioflavonoids, cofactors and micronutrients that food offers.

### Vitamin A and Beta-Carotene
- Beta-carotene converts into vitamin A (retinol) in the body.
- Where you can find it: sweet potatoes, carrots, dark leafy greens, butternut squash, romaine lettuce, dried apricots, cantaloupe
- What it does for the body: protects vision, immune health, skin health
- Symptoms of excess: jaundice, nausea, hair loss
- Symptoms of deficiency: blindness in extreme cases

### Riboflavin (Vitamin B2)
- Where you can find it: cheese, almonds, lean beef, lamb, salmon, eggs, pork, mushrooms, sesame seeds
- What it does for the body: improve energy metabolism
- Symptoms of excess: adverse cellular effects
- Symptoms of deficiency: dry lips, sore throat, anemia

### Niacin (Vitamin B3)
- Where you can find it: tuna fish, chicken, turkey, peanuts, mushrooms, green peas, sunflower seeds, avocado
- What it does for the body: lowers cholesterol, regulates blood sugar, processes fat
- Symptoms of excess: skin rashes or flushes, dry skin
- Symptoms of deficiency: anxiety, fatigue, depression, dementia

### Pyridoxine (Vitamin B6)
- Where you can find it: bananas, cereal grains, carrots, spinach, peas, potatoes
- What it does for the body: adrenal function, nervous system health, metabolic processing
- Symptoms of excess: nerve damage, numbness and tingling
- Symptoms of deficiency: dermatitis, cracked lips, inflamed mouth, depression, insomnia

### Cobalamin (Vitamin B12)

- Where you can find it: shellfish, tofu, meat, cheese, eggs
- What it does for the body: maintains nerve and blood health
- Symptoms of excess: numbness and tingling
- Symptoms of deficiency: anemia, fatigue, depression

### Vitamin C

- Where you can find it: Citrus fruits, berries, broccoli, cauliflower, Brussels sprouts, leafy greens
- What it does for the body: helps build and maintain connective tissue and bones, helps balance free radicals
- Symptoms of excess: nausea, heartburn, headache
- Symptoms of deficiency: anemia, gingivitis and bleeding gums, inflamed joints, dry hair and skin, slowed metabolism, decreased ability to fight disease and infection, fatigue

### Vitamin D

- Where you can find it: cod liver oil, smoked salmon, mushrooms, tofu, eggs
- What it does for the body: required by the body for the absorption of calcium, assists bone development and immune function, alleviates inflammation
- Symptoms of excess: kidney stones, increased risk of heart disease
- Symptoms of deficiency: rickets, weak immune system, poor hair growth

### Vitamin E

- Where you can find it: dark leafy greens, almonds, hazelnuts, pistachios, sunflower seeds, avocados
- What it does for the body: helps prevent oxidative stress
- Symptoms of excess: excessive bleeding or hemorrhaging
- Symptoms of deficiency: chronic liver disease, neurological damage

### Vitamin K

- Where you can find it: leafy greens, Brussels sprouts
- What it does for the body: regulates clotting
- Symptoms of excess: may interfere with blood thinning/thickening medications
- Symptoms of deficiency: uncontrolled bleeding, defective blood clotting, osteoporosis

### Enzymes

Enzymes are not only essential for digestion, they're vital for virtually every process in your body. This includes gut health and healing, pathogen control and immune support. We'll cover enzymes in more detail in a later chapter, but for now understand there are three main types of enzymes: digestive, metabolic and food based.

Digestive and metabolic enzymes are produced by your pancreas, but you will need to eat *raw food* to obtain food-based enzymes. Since heating food above 116 °F (46 °C) kills the enzymes, it is critical to eat these foods raw to benefit from their enzymes.

Enzyme deficiency causes poor digestion and an inability to absorb important nutrients. Symptoms include constipation, bloating and heartburn plus an inability to absorb nutrients can lead to any number of illnesses.

The amount of enzymes your body produces changes as you age. Every ten years, enzyme production decreases by ten to fifteen percent. Thus, getting sufficient enzymes from food is an increasingly important factor in holistic health and wellness throughout your life.

**Foods rich in enzymes:**

- Organic Papaya
- Organic Avocado
- Raw Honey
- Organic Extra Virgin Olive Oil
- Organic Coconut Oil

## KEY POINTS:

- Chew your food. When you chew, digestive enzymes are released in your saliva to start the digestion process.

- Avoid chewing gum, which fakes your body into thinking you are eating and you expends digestive enzymes unnecessarily.

- Eat some raw food on a daily basis.

# pH, Alkalinity and Acidity

pH (the potential of Hydrogen) is a measure of the body's overall alkalinity or acidity. On a pH scale, higher readings are more alkaline and oxygen-rich while lower readings indicate are more acidic and oxygen-poor. You can test your pH through saliva, blood or urine tests.

**Human blood pH always strives for a slightly alkaline state (7.35-7.45).**
To reach this state, you want to eat primarily alkalizing foods (70-80% of your diet) and less acidic foods (20%-30% of your diet). If your diet is unbalanced, it is likely causing an imbalance in pH. In other words, if you eat a diet heavy in meats, carbs and sugars and have a more acidic pH, your body works harder to neutralize its pH to safely remove the acids from your body. To do this, your body has to utilize minerals and energy from other organs, pulling itself away from other important work which causes strain. It takes energy away from healing and thriving.

**What causes an acidic pH?**

- Emotional stress
- Toxins
- Too much acidic food (pickled vegetables, meats, coffee)

| | Acidic – Alkaline | | | | | | | | | |
|---|---|---|---|---|---|---|---|---|---|---|
| | - 5.0 | 5.5 | 6.0 | 6.5 | 7.0 | 7.5 | 8.0 | 8.5 | 9.0 | 9.5 + |
| **Food Category** | Highly Acidic | | Acidic | | Close to Neutral | | Alkaline | | Highly Alkaline | |
| Fruits | Canned fruit | | Fruit juices | | Coconut, sour cherries, avocados, strawberries, bananas, blueberries, cranberries | | Apples, pears, kiwis, grapes, dates, citrus fruits | | Dried fruit | |
| Vegetables | Pickled vegetables | | Sweet potatoes, steamed spinach | | Squash, asparagus, mushrooms, onion, cabbage, peas, cauliflower, potatoes, olives | | Carrots, green beans, beets, lettuce, zucchini | | Vegetable juices, raw spinach, broccoli, celery, garlic, parsley | |
| Legumes | | | Pinto and navy beans | | Kidney beans | | Lima beans | | | |
| Meats | Beef, pork, veal, shellfish, canned tuna, sardines | | Fish, turkey, chicken, lamb | | Oysters, organ meats | | | | | |
| Beverages | Black tea, coffee, liquor | | Wine, soda | | Cocoa, ginger tea | | Green tea | | Herbal teas, lemon water | |

## The Inflammation Factor

Inflammation is not the devil. It is information. Inflammation is a natural part of the healing process. The problem with inflammation occurs when we get stuck in the inflammatory response. Too much inflammation that fails to subside naturally is one common source of chronic pain. Therefore, when you are in a state of chronic pain, one of your main objectives should be to reduce 'stuck' inflammation.

### Top foods to avoid when trying to reduce inflammation:

- White Sugar
- White Bread
- White Rice
- Tomatoes
- Hydrogenated fats (Trans-Fats)
- Monosodium glutamate (MSG)
- All artificial sweeteners
- Excess alcohol

### Foods that cause inflammation and pain:

**Nightshades**

- Several nightshades are toxic and even deadly (belladonna), but others are edible. Edible nightshades can contribute to inflammation and pain. For most people they are ok to eat in a balanced diet, but should be avoided for those who are experiencing pain or chronic health conditions. If you are struggling with an autoimmune disorder, chronic inflammation, arthritis, or have a digestive sensitivity, you may want to try eliminating nightshades from your diet for several months to see how you feel without them.

- Edible nightshades to **avoid** when fighting inflammation-based pain include:
  - Potatoes
  - Tomatoes
  - Sweet peppers
  - Hot peppers
  - Paprika
  - Red pepper flakes
  - Cayenne
  - Eggplant

**Sugar**

- Processed sugars create inflammation by triggering the release of cytokines.

- When reading ingredient lists, be aware that several items ending with 'ose' is a form of processed sugar.

- Common sugars on ingredient lists to **avoid** include:
  - Fructose
  - Sucrose
  - Glucose
  - Barley Malt
  - Maltose
  - Dextrose
  - Rice Syrup
  - Agave (has more concentrated sugar than high fructose corn syrup)

### Alkaloids

- Alkaloids are chemical compounds that operate naturally within plants to repel insects. Their job is to kill the bad intruders. They are often found in the leaves, stems and other parts of the nightshade plants that we do not normally eat. They are found in such small amounts they typically won't affect a person who is in good health. But they can cause irritation for someone whose immune system is compromised. For example, if you have an autoimmune disorder and your digestive system is already struggling, alkaloids in your food will continue their job of 'killing' the bad guys in your intestines which can contribute to leaky gut and other digestive maladies.

- Alkaloids include:
  - Solanine: found in potatoes especially in green potatoes and mostly in the skin
  - Nicotine: is found in many nightshades plants (in small amounts)
  - Capsaicin: found in peppers; capsaicin gives peppers their heat. The higher the alkaloid content, the more inflammation is caused.

- To reduce your alkaloid intake:
  - peel potato skins
  - avoid unripe nightshades (like green tomatoes or sprouting potatoes)
  - Cook nightshade vegetables if you eat them, which reduces the amount of alkaloids in them

### Gluten

- Gluten, comprised of the proteins glutenin and gliadin, plays a major role in both inflammation and pain. Gliadin, which helps bread rise during baking, creates most of the negative health consequences of gluten.

- Although some people tolerate gluten well, others have a sensitivity to it. For those trying to heal chronic pain, gluten should be avoided.

- The most recognized disease associated with gluten is celiac disease, when the exposure to gluten causes a damaging immune response in the small intestine. Untreated, celiac disease prevent the body from absorbing nutrients properly, causing iron deficiency, osteoporosis and more. A blood test can help you determine if you have celiac disease versus a less threatening wheat allergy.

- Irritable bowel syndrome (IBS), schizophrenia and autism are other disorders that could benefit from a gluten-free diet.

- Foods high in gluten include but are not limited to: wheat, spelt, barley, rye, breads, pastries, cookies, cakes, pastas, beer and cereals.

- Check for gluten in food products on ingredients lists.

- Gluten-free grain alternatives to try include: amaranth, buckwheat, grits (corn), quinoa, millet, oats, coconut flour, almond flour, chia and wild rice.

| Symptoms of Gluten Sensitivities | | | | |
|---|---|---|---|---|
| Abdominal pain | Bloating | Constipation | Depression / anxiety | Autoimmune disorders |
| Joint pain | Chronic fatigue | Migraine headaches | ADHD | Weight gain / loss |
| Muscle aches | Diarrhea | "Brain fog" | Low immunity | Eczema / acne / psoriasis |

If you suffer from any of these, take action. Get tested for gluten sensitivities.

| Foods That Contain Gluten | | | | |
|---|---|---|---|---|
| Wheat Starch | Durum | Fu* | Semolina | Rye |
| Wheat Bran | Einkorn | Gliadin | Spelt | Seitan |
| Wheat Germ | Emmer | Graham Flour | Barley | Triticale and Mir*** |
| Couscous | Farina | Kamut | Bulgur | |
| Cracked Wheat | Faro | Matzo | Oats** | |

- \* Common in Asian foods
- \*\* Oats themselves don't contain gluten, but are often processed in plants that produce gluten-containing grains and may be contaminated
- \*\*\* A cross between wheat and rye

Unless specifically marked as gluten-free, prepackaged foods may or may not have gluten as equipment may be shared for multiple ingredients. At a minimum, always check the ingredients list on the nutrition facts label for these common sources of gluten.

If you have a gluten allergy, you will also want to avoid foods and sauces that have been made in the same pan with any gluten-containing food. Gluten may also be found in ingredients such as barley malt, beers, wines, chicken broth, malt vinegar, salad dressings, spice mixes, veggie burgers and soy sauce.

**Allergens**

- When the immune system feels it is under attack from an allergen or CIC (circulating immune complex), it responds by thrusting itself into the healing process by releasing antibodies and creating inflammation.

- Acute allergic responses are the initial responses your body has to anything it feels is attacking it. While different people are allergic to different things, symptoms for allergic reactions can be similar. These symptoms can include redness, puffiness, itchiness and irritation.

- Chronic allergic responses such as asthma attacks can be due to prolonged inflammation.

- Severe allergic reactions should not wait for home remedies. In the case of extreme allergic reactions, get medical help as quickly as possible.
- Do not confuse allergic inflammation with infection, as they should be treated differently.

**Lectins**

- Lectins are a family of proteins found in all foods (both plants and animals). Some foods have more lectins than others, and some lectins are more harmful than others. Concentrated amounts of lectins (excess) can contribute to inflammation, pain and digestive issues.
- Lectins' role in plants vary. They defend the plant against pests and they also help seeds stay intact as they travel through the animals' digestive systems.
- Similar to animals, we do not digest lectins. Because we do not digest them, our bodies produce antibodies to them which causes an immune system response.
- Uncooked, raw legumes (such as kidney beans) have the most amount of lectins, followed by grains, dairy, seafood and plants.
- An excess of lectins can cause any of the problems associated with inflammation and immune responses including but not limited to: skin rashes, joint pain, flatulence, nausea, vomiting and diarrhea.
- Top food allergens are also high in lectins: dairy, wheat, eggs, tree nuts, peanuts, soy, fish and shellfish.
- Lectins cannot be avoided altogether. However, there are some best practices you can use when considering lectins in your diet:
  - Choose sprouts. Most sprouts are lower in lectins. The longer the grain, seed or bean has sprouted, the more lectins are deactivated. Alfalfa sprouts are an exception as sprouting has the opposite effect, increasing their lectin content.
  - Soak grains and beans overnight. This, along with boiling during cooking, reduces lectins. Pro tip: add a little baking soda to your soaking water to reduce lectins even further.
  - Eat fermented, probiotic foods. Fermentation reduces lectins. Examples of foods you can ferment and eat include tofu, miso, tempeh, tamari, cabbage and sourdough. You can also make your own fermented foods using Saccharomyces Boulardii (S. Boulardii). S. Boulardii are the peacekeepers of the probiotic families and available in most health food stores and natural pharmacies.
  - Eat prebiotic foods.to feed the good bacteria and enhance gut health. Examples of prebiotic foods are raw garlic, raw onions, raw leeks, and raw asparagus.

**Herbicides and Pesticides**

- Designed to keep pests off of vegetables and fruits, herbicides and pesticides are harmful to your body in many ways:
    - They disrupt the body's ability to break down estrogen and testosterone.
    - They affect the endocrine glands: adrenals, thyroid, pituitary, ovaries and testes
    - Long-term exposure has caused problems in utero such as deformed reproductive anatomies, defects in sperm counts, defects in metabolism and impaired brain development.
    - They have been linked to autism and ADHD.
    - They have been linked to various cancers.
- How can you minimize pesticide exposure?
    - Buy local, organic fruits and vegetables when possible.
    - Wash and scrub fruits and vegetables before eating with non toxic washes.
    - Grow an organic home garden.
    - Remove the outer layer of fruits and vegetables when possible, such as the outer leaves of cabbage or lettuce.

**GMOs**

- GMOs, or genetically modified organisms, are created in a laboratory setting when foreign genes from one species are extracted and artificially imposed into the genes of another species. The foreign genes may come from bacteria, viruses, insects, animals or even humans. Because GMOs are herbicide tolerant, toxic herbicide use has increased in these crops making them doubly problematic.
- Most conventionally grown crops in the United States now have some genetic modifications. Many are not labeled.
- Common GMO foods to be aware of:
    - Soy
    - Corn
    - Cotton
    - Canola
    - Sugar beets
    - Alfalfa
    - Aspartame
    - Dairy
- **How can you avoid GMOs?**
    - Look for products that are labeled USDA Certified Organic.
    - Avoid products not specifically labeled as non-GMO.

**Bad Fats**

- Unsaturated fats are good for you: they help lower cholesterol levels and risk of heart disease.

- Saturated and trans fats, however, are highly inflammatory and more likely to cause pain and health complications.

- Use anti-inflammatory olive oil instead of saturated fats like lard while cooking. Other healthy fats/oils to use while cooking include grapeseed oil, macadamia nut oil, polyunsaturated fats and omega-3 fats from fish.

**How to make the change**

- Detox your body. (See Cleansing and Detoxing chapter)

- Clean up your diet using the tips above.

- Make choices you know from a gut feeling are right for you.

- Stay consistent with change–incremental changes you stick with produce better long-term results than big changes you abandon in a week or two.

## KEY POINTS:

- Meal planning helps create a balanced diet. A balanced diet includes proper nutrition, which helps eliminate inflammation and pain over time.

- Enzymes help you absorb nutrients, maintain gut health and reduce inflammation throughout your body. You need more as you get older. Get more in your diet by eating some raw food every day.

- pH matters. Eat three alkalizing foods for each acidic food choice (75% versus 25%).

- Eat organic foods when possible, always taking time to wash and scrub fruits and vegetables before eating.

## Food Requirements for Optimal Healing

If you are in a state of chronic pain, this indicates you are out of balance somewhere physically, nutritionally, mentally, spiritually or some combination of those.

To restore nutritional balance, you will have different dietary requirements than a person of good health already in balance. Below we address the nutritional requirements you'll want to follow for optimal healing.

## Calories and Sources

During a healing crisis, after surgery, or following a major workout, your body goes into repair mode. During this time you will require 10% to 20% more calories than normal. Getting those calories from good sources in the right proportion is crucial for healing and recovery. Stop eating processed foods during this time and focus on eating whole fruits, vegetables and lean proteins.

Rather than three large meals, try eating smaller meals five to six times per day. You need approximately:

- 5 protein servings per day (20 to 30 grams each)

  Example: 3 to 4 eggs or 3 to 4 ounces of meat

- 2 vegetable servings per day (1 to 2 cups each)

  Example: 1 cup raw or cooked veggies, 1 cup pure veggie juice, or 2 cups raw leafy greens

- 2 fruit servings per day (1/2 cup to 1 cup each)

  Example: 1 cup fresh fruit, ½ cup dried fruit

## Fats

Not all fats are bad. In fact, fat-soluble vitamins (A, D, E, K and carotenoids) need fat in order to be absorbed into your bloodstream. When eaten in balance, fats supply energy to your body. When eaten in excess or deficiency your body cannot operate at its prime.

There are two main types of fats: saturated and unsaturated. Unsaturated fats are known as the 'good' fats, found in foods like avocados, nuts and healthy oils such as olive oil. Saturated fats are known as the 'bad' fats. When eaten in excess and without a balanced diet, saturated fats contribute to heart disease. However, when eaten properly they can help brain health and quelch fake hunger thoughts produced by the limbic system, or emotional part of the brain, when it thinks it is hungry.

Like everything we teach you in this book, balance is the key. Both saturated and unsaturated fats are needed as part of a healthy diet. Striking the right balance in how much you consume is crucial for optimal health and to break out of the inflammatory pain cycle.

### Eating Fat for Weight Loss and Muscle Growth

While we do not support or refute any specific diets, we mention some of them as positive learning options. In the Bulletproof Diet, acclaimed biohacker Dave Asprey makes an effort to help people live optimally through a diet high in healthy fats, vegetables, carbs and proteins paired with intermittent fasting.

On his plan, general ranges for healthy fat intake go as high as 50% to 80% fat in your diet, while he leaves 5% to 30% for carbohydrates and 10% to 30% for proteins. This may sound shocking at first, since the suggested fat intake is significantly more than we hear about in most modern dietary plans. However, his plan includes eating the above ratios only during a 6- to 8-hour window. Limiting the window of time you eat, also understood as intermittent fasting, has certain benefits such as putting your body into a metabolic process known as ketosis. In ketosis, your body will use fats for energy instead of carbs.

| | Saturated Fats | Unsaturated Fats | | | | | | |
|---|---|---|---|---|---|---|---|---|
| | | Trans Fats | Monounsaturated Fats | Polyunsaturated Fats | | | | |
| | | | | Omega-3 Essential EPA*, DHA** | Omega-5 Essential Punicic acid | Omega-6 Essential gamma-linolenic acid | Omega-7 Non-essential Palmitoleic Acid | Omega-9 Non-essential Oleic Acid |
| **Sources** | Animal meats Butter Milk Cheese Cacao bean Coconut oil Palm oil | Junk foods, boxed foods, processed food products<br><br>Trans fats are listed as "hydrogenated" or "partially hydrogenated" | Plant-based oils Nuts and seeds Olive oil Olives Avocados Red meats Whole milk products | Cold water, fatty fish including sardines, salmon, mackerel and tuna, krill, some brands of eggs are omega-3 fortified<br><br>ALA, alpha-linoleic acid is sourced from plants including flax, hemp and chia | Pomegranate seeds | Chicken, beef, pork, nuts, grains, seeds and vegetable oils | Cold water, fatty fish including salmon, tuna, mackerel and trout; non-animal sources include macadamia nuts and sea buckthorn berries | Non-essential means our bodies make this on its own; sourced from olive, canola, peanut and sunflower oils |
| **Should you eat it?** | Yes, essential for cell membranes and hormone production | No, you should never eat these fats, in any amount ever | Yes, but choose wisely as some of the plant-based oils are better than others | Yes, but see Appendix C | Clinical research around the world is very promising, so If you like pomegranates have at it, supplements are limited at this point in time | Yes, but see Appendix A | Yes, but research suggests you most likely get enough omega-7s while eating for omega-3s | There are several different oil choices, we prefer olive oil over any other |
| **Limits** | < 20g Daily | 0g Daily | 24g Daily | 20g Daily for all Polyunsaturated fats | | | | |

*eicosapentaenoic acid
**docosahexaenoic acid

## How much fat should I get in my diet?

The amount of fat you should eat varies for each person. For most people, a good rule of thumb is to keep fats between 20% to 35% of your daily caloric intake. For someone eating a 2,000 calorie/day diet, that means 400 to 700 calories should come from healthy fats.

Here are some estimates to help you determine how much **saturated fat** you could eat based on a 2,000 calorie/day diet:

- 1 ounce of organic cheddar cheese = 6 grams of saturated fat (114 calories)
- 1 cup of whole raw milk = 4.6 grams of saturated fat (146 calories)
- 1 teaspoon of organic grassfed butter = 2.4 grams of saturated fat (34 calories)
- 3 ounces organic, free range, hormone free, grassfed ground beef = 6.1 grams of saturated fat (212 calories)
- 3 ounces of baked, wild caught fish = 1.5 grams of saturated fat (129 calories)

Here are some estimates to help you determine how much **unsaturated fat** you could eat based on a 2,000 calorie/day diet:

- 1 avocado = 20 grams of unsaturated fat (236 calories)
- ½ cup walnuts = 25 grams of unsaturated fat (260 calories)
- ½ cup olives = 7.5 grams of unsatruated fat (75 calories)

## Proteins

Once digested, protein turns into amino acids which promotes healing. When you are in a healing state, you need a little more protein than normal. This is why athletes drink protein shakes after their workout. Protein requirements range from 6 to 12 ounces per day, or .5 to 1.2 grams of protein per pound of body weight.

It is also important to consider the type of fat you are getting with each serving of protein. If you are doing a great job of getting protein through peanut butter and beef which contain omega-6 fatty acids, but never eat fish or seafood which contain omega-3 fatty acids, you will create an imbalance of fatty acids. Bottom line: if you do not eat seafood, you are not getting omega-3 fatty acids and will need to supplement.

Let's break this down a little further in a scenario where a 150-pound person wishes to eat an average 150 grams of protein per day over the course of 5 to 6 meals and snacks per day.

- Eat 20 to 30 grams of protein at each meal/snack.
- Eat a variety of proteins with omega-6 fatty acids (beef, poultry, pork, eggs, nuts, dairy) as well as those that contain omega-3 fatty acids (seafood).

- Each of the items listed below have approximately 20 to 30 grams of protein:
  - 3 to 4 eggs
  - 3 to 4 ounces salmon
  - 3 to 4 ounces peanut butter
  - 3 to 4 ounces chicken
  - 1 to 1 ½ cups hummus

## Carbohydrates

Your body needs carbohydrates to turn the protein you eat into fuel. Without carbs, your body spends energy burning the protein instead of spending the energy on fueling healing.

We are not talking about refined carbohydrates from sources such as processed breads and crackers. In excess (or if you have an allergy), refined carbs are known to cause chronic conditions such as leaky gut, insulin resistance and impaired cognitive function.

Unrefined carbohydrates like potatoes, whole grains, and raw fruits and vegetables are a good source of healing energy for your body. While you are trying to heal from pain, increase your intake of plant-based unrefined carbohydrates to give your body the energy it needs to carry out healing tasks.

## Bone Health

Bones give us our structure and form. Maintaining strong bones in a lifetime process and bone health is critical to recovery from muscular or cartilage injuries. You will not be able to grow good cartilage or repair muscles if your bones are weak. Take care of them by getting proper nutrition from food and supplementing with vitamins and minerals when necessary.

Your bones require at least 13 key nutrients to remain strong, including vitamins C, D3, K and several from the B family plus calcium, magnesium, silicon, strontium, vanadium, phosphorus, zinc, copper and boron. Males typically need a little more than females, but each person has different health concerns to consider regarding dosage.

## Stay Hydrated While Healing

Under normal circumstances, we should drink 1 to 1.5 ounces of water for every pound of body weight. For example, if you weigh 150 pounds, you should drink 150+ ounces of water each day. While healing, it is especially important to stay hydrated so everything can function properly.

### Power Vitamins and Minerals to Boost Bone Strength

The Calcium Lie by Dr. Robert Thompson and Kathleen Barnes is a valuable resource for understanding bone health. They explain how calcium alone will not strengthen bones. Instead, at least 13 different nutrients are required. Again, always aim to get your vital nutrients from food first, then add any minerals and supplements as needed.

# EAT FRESH AND
# DITCH THE PROCESSED
# "FRANKENFOODS"

Food keeps us alive. We need it to heal and grow. Without it we would die. It's also true that the better we eat, the better our health. But *what* should you eat?

We live in a time where advancements in science and technology regarding food have become both a blessing and a curse. The task of eating the right foods can get so confusing it may cause someone to stop caring about what they eat. The purpose of this book is to help you more easily navigate this information about food so you can take control of your health through one of the few things you will do for the rest of your life: eat.

## Food Choices

Working with the concept of The Complete Healing Formula™ to identify imbalances and aiming to rebalance the body, these important factors need to be considered:

### Understanding the Term "Whole Foods"

Whole foods are foods that have not been processed or refined. These provide a full range of nutrients. Fruits, vegetables, animal proteins, beans and unrefined / unprocessed grains are all whole foods.

### All Natural vs Organic

All natural refers to food that is fresh out of the ground or off the vine. All natural food is typically considered to be unprocessed. One concern with all natural food is the U.S. Department of Agriculture does not monitor or regulate 'all natural' labels. This means any food seller can label their products as being 'all natural' even if they contain heavily processed ingredients. A food containing red food coloring made from insects, for example, can be labeled all natural. Organic is a much better choice. Food must meet strict regulations to be labeled organic. Organic food contains no antibiotics or hormones, no toxic synthetic pesticides or herbicides, and no chemical fertilizers.

There is no legal definition of "Natural." However, products labeled "Organic" must follow a strict third-party verification system that regulates feed production and processing:

- To be labeled 100% USDA Organic, products must be 100% Organic.
- Products that are 95% Organic can still be labeled Organic.
- Products that are 70% Organic can say "made with organic ingredients" on their label.
- Products that are less than 70% organic cannot use the seal on their label, but they can include organic items in the ingredient list.

| Standards Required | Organic | Natural |
| --- | --- | --- |
| Farm production annually inspected by third-party certification agency | YES | NO |
| Humane treatment of livestock | YES | N/A |
| Livestock eat certified Organic feed | YES | NO |
| Livestock feed does not contain rendered animal byproducts | YES | N/A |
| GMOs prohibited in food production | YES | NO |
| Sewage sludge prohibited in food production | YES | NO |
| Irradiation prohibited in food production | YES | NO |
| Livestock are fed feed that does not contain pesticides | YES | N/A |
| Livestock are fed feed that does not contain herbicides | YES | N/A |
| Livestock are fed feed that does not contain synthetic fertilizers | YES | N/A |
| Livestock are raised without antibiotics or growth hormones | YES | N/A |
| Livestock have access to pasture | YES | N/A |
| Livestock are finished on family farms (not commercial feedlots) | YES | N/A |

## Organic vs Synthetic

Organic is natural while synthetic is man-made. Always choose organic foods over synthetic when possible.

## GMO vs Hybrid vs Organic Seeds

'GMO' seeds, or genetically modified organisms, are produced in a laboratory. They cross two different plant varieties or sometimes completely different organisms such as a bacteria and a plant to create a new product. GMO seeds create plants that are somewhat unknown territory. These "Frankenfoods" are unnatural and more likely to cause harm and imbalance in your health.

A hybrid seed refers to selective breeding of two similar plants to create an improved variety. This practice dates back to the mid-nineteenth century. Done once, it seems to be fine. The problem occurs when you take the second generation plant's seeds and assume they will reproduce a similar version of themselves. The second generation plants do not carry the intended improvements. There is nothing inherently wrong with first-generation hybrid seeds. It is low tech and can be done simply without drastically altering the nutrients and properties of the plant. One downside of using hybrid seeds is it keeps you reliant on seed companies for the first generation hybrid seeds as opposed to replanting seeds from your own plants and continuing to grow them.

The best choice is to use organic seeds that can be reproduced through their own natural lifecycle.

### Raw food vs Processed Food

Raw food is unprocessed and in a natural state while processed foods have undergone some type of man-made processing. For example, you can buy a fresh whole tomato or you can buy canned tomatoes. The first is raw, the latter processed. In most cases raw is a better, healthier choice although certain preserved foods will retain their nutrient qualities. This is where reading labels becomes important. We'll explain how to understand the nutrition facts labels found on processed foods later in this chapter. When in doubt, fresh (or raw) is best.

### Food vs Food Product

Vegetables, fruits and animal proteins are all considered food. Food products are synthetically made food items such as cheetos or gummi bears. Food is always better for you than food products.

### Wild Caught vs Farm-raised Fish

Farm-raised fish often gets a bad rap as harvested from small water tanks where the fish are not in fresh, clean water. It could be argued that wild caught fish also come from contaminated waters. So which is the better choice?

Wild caught is a better choice than farm-raised which tends to be higher in contaminants, lower in many nutrients and likely to contain more saturated fat the wild caught fish have a chance to swim off in open waters. That said, some fisheries now raise fish in open waters using sustainable, natural methods resulting in healthier fish for consumption than those raised in tanks.

Be sure to ask your fish purveyor or grocery store where the fish was harvested from, when it was caught, and whether it was harvested using sustainable methods. Fish caught in the

### Did you know?

Farm-raised fish like tilapia are sometimes fed a diet of "particulates" which include those found in wastewater (e.g. poop). It may not be directly harmful but it's certainly not appetizing.

Atlantic at the time of the writing of this book is a better choice than Pacific-caught fish due to high levels of toxic and radioactive chemicals present following the 2011 nuclear disaster in Japan.

Avoid eating overfished species by researching the Monterey Bay Aquarium Seafood Watch (www.seafoodwatch.org) or the Environmental Defense Fund Seafood Selector (seafood.edf.org). When given the option to choose either internationally-harvested fish or United States-harvested fish, keep in mind the United States has the strictest environmental and food safety laws regarding wild caught and farm-raised fish.

## Fermented vs Unfermented Soy

Soy products like soy milk, soy sauce and tofu are made from soybeans, which are a legume. Soybeans are a source of protein, omega-3 fatty acids, tryptophan, fiber, iron and various other minerals and nutrients. The soybean in its natural form is healthier than any processed soy product, many of which have toxic levels of aluminum and manganese due to being washed in aluminum tanks during processing.

Soy food products can be made with fermented soy such as miso, tempeh and soy sauce, or unfermented soy such as most tofus and soy milk. Fermentation is a natural process that does not decrease the nutritional value like high heat processing does. Unfermented soy contains phytic acid, which blocks absorption of minerals the hormonal glands need for proper function. Fermentation removes the phytic acid and eliminates concerns about harming the hormonal system.

Another consideration when eating unfermented, manufactured soy is the amount of phytoestrogens it contains. When soy is manufactured, natural phytoestrogens are converted to toxic xenoestrogens, which mimic the female hormone estrogen. Eating too much unfermented, manufactured soy is extremely detrimental to your hormonal system. The same is not true for fermented soy. However, like any food, eat soy in moderation and in balance with a variety of other foods, choosing fermented soy over unfermented soy when possible.

Also note: eating soy increases your body's requirement for vitamins D3 and B12.

If you are watching your soy intake, be sure to read the ingredients and nutrition facts label. When eating out, be aware several cooking products the restaurant may use contain soy that the waiter/waitress may not know about. For example, soy lecithin is a common ingredient to be aware of when attempting to limit processed soy.

Watch out for manufactured soy in products such as:

- Herbal teas–may contain soy lecithin
- Sodas–may contain brominated vegetable oil which may come from soy
- Instant oatmeal–may contain soy protein isolate or partially hydrogenated soy oil

- Soy candles and artificial fire logs–You may want to steer away from these if you have a soy allergy or have built up too much soy in your system

For more information on soy, we highly recommend reviewing the resources on the Weston A. Price Foundation's Soy Alert! page: www.westonaprice.org/soy-alert

## Isolate vs Concentrate

The majority of soy products such as soy hot dogs, soy nuggets, soy ice cream and soy cheese are highly processed and made with a soy protein isolate as opposed to the natural soybean. Isolates are a bland white powder which are absorbed faster when taken in supplement form. Soy isolate is void of fiber and nutrients but high in protein. Soy concentrate is made by extracting the oil and sugars from soybean meal meaning ti keeps the added benefit of more fiber, protein and nutrients than soy isolate.

## KEY POINTS:

- You always have dietary choices to make but eating healthy narrows your food focus.

- Don't let the number of options overwhelm you. Follow the guidelines in this book to simplify your dietary decision-making process to navigate your health to a balanced state.

## Role of Supplements

As the name implies, supplements help fill any nutritional gaps in your diet. These dietary vitamins, minerals, amino acids, enzymes, herbs and various other nutrient dense sources can be found in capsule, tablet, tincture and liquid form. When you have imbalances caused by insufficiencies in your daily nutritional requirements, carefully selected supplements help rebalance your system.

While all supplement manufacturers are regulated by the Food and Drug Administration, supplements are not regulated like drugs because they are considered to be food in the United States under the Dietary Supplement Health and Education Act of 1994.

Well-sourced food may have enough nutrients to keep you healthy, but sometimes you need extra help. Supplements are intended to support your diet, not replace it.

When deciding whether to add supplements to your diet, remember: food first. There are phytonutrients, co-factors and bioflavanoids found in foods that simply are not included in supplements. Start with the right foods then add supplements as needed to help support and maintain nutritional balance.

## Nutrition Facts Labels

In addition to the ingredients list, the nutrition facts label is your key to understanding the packaged food you are considering purchasing and eating.

**The serving size** indicates the amount (or size) of one serving. All of the nutritional data including calories, fats, proteins, and vitamins are calculated based on the serving size.

**The number of servings** per container indicates how many servings are in the package based on the serving size. If the serving size is one cup, and there are two servings in the product, then the product contains two cups. Note that in this case all of the nutritional data would need to be doubled to calculate how much nutrition is in the entire package compared to a single serving size.

**Calories** indicate the amount of calories per serving and the **calories from fat** are also noted here. Be aware that low fat and fat-free products are not calorie-free.

**Fats, cholesterol and sodium** are shown in grams and percent daily values, with the exception of trans fats. When comparing products, select the one with lower saturated fat, trans fat, cholesterol and sodium. The percent daily value for total fats is the sum of all of the fats included in the product.

**Dietary fiber and sugars** are calculated as **carbohydrates.** There is no percent daily value calculated for sugars. While natural sugar from fruit is good, added sugars such as high fructose corn syrup or glucose increase inflammation and pain.

**Protein** indicates how many grams of protein are in one serving. Remember to get protein from a variety of sources for a good mix of omega-3s and omega-6s.

**Vitamins and minerals** are listed with a percent daily value as well. When comparing products, choose the one with the highest ratio of vitamins and minerals to calories.

# Nutrition Facts

Serving Size 2/3 cup (55g)
Servings Per Container About 8

**Amount Per Serving**

| **Calories** 230 | Calories from Fat 40 |
|---|---|

| | **% Daily Value*** |
|---|---|
| **Total Fat** 8g | **12%** |
| Saturated Fat 1g | **5%** |
| *Trans* Fat 0g | |
| **Cholesterol** 0mg | **0%** |
| **Sodium** 160mg | **7%** |
| **Total Carbohydrate** 37g | **12%** |
| Dietary Fiber 4g | **16%** |
| Sugars 1g | |
| **Protein** 3g | |
| | |
| Vitamin A | 10% |
| Vitamin C | 8% |
| Calcium | 20% |
| Iron | 45% |

* Percent Daily Values are based on a 2,000 calorie diet. Your daily value may be higher or lower depending on your calorie needs.

| | Calories: | 2,000 | 2,500 |
|---|---|---|---|
| Total Fat | Less than | 65g | 80g |
| Sat Fat | Less than | 20g | 25g |
| Cholesterol | Less than | 300mg | 300mg |
| Sodium | Less than | 2,400mg | 2,400mg |
| Total Carbohydrate | | 300g | 375g |
| Dietary Fiber | | 25g | 30g |

**Percent daily values** help you estimate how much of any particular nutrient you get per serving based on a 2,000-calorie-per-day diet. Less than 5% is considered low while 20% or more is considered high.

# Good Health Begins in the Gut

## Essential Supplements for Digestion and Gut Health

The bigger picture of why we are talking about food, nutritional values, supplements, and digestion is that in order to regulate inflammation, heal our bodies and become pain free, your digestive system must continuously operate at an optimal level. So let's take a quick look at our digestive system and what your body requires for peak performance.

The first component is enzymes. Enzymes are catalysts that speed up the breakdown of all of the different food groups. Without enzymes, digestion and absorption would not happen fast enough to keep us alive. In other words, we would starve to death waiting for our food to be utilized without enzymes. Next are hormones, which stimulate the essential secretions, gastrin, secretin and CCK needed to protect and digest food matter. Third is mucus, which protects and lubricates the digestive system.

A happy, healthy and active body greatly supports good digestion and absorption. However, there will always be the possibility our bodies may be operating with imbalances in our hormones, saliva, bile, gut flora, fiber and what we feel is the most important digestive component of all, enzymes.

## What are Enzymes?

Enzymes are tiny proteins that speed up the biochemical processes in our bodies. There are an estimated 75,000 different enzymes said to exist in the human body, all responsible for specific actions to help our bodies grow, heal and maintain an optimal state of being.

### The different types of enzymes:

Of all those enzymes, there are only three categories:

1. Metabolic (or systemic) enzymes that help our bodies function.

2. Digestive enzymes that help break down our food making it easier to absorb.

3. Plant / food-based enzymes naturally found in uncooked and unprocessed foods that start our foods' digestion.

## Where Do Enzymes Come From?

The enzymes our bodies can utilize come from four separate sources: enzymes our bodies produce on their own, plant-based enzymes, animal-sourced enzymes and fungal-based enzymes.

- **What we produce naturally:** Our pancreas is the primary organ that produces our digestive and metabolic enzymes. However, as we age the organs and glands that produce these enzymes produce less and less enzymes (both digestive and metabolic). This is why enzyme supplementation could be the missing link to your recovery, especially as you grow older.

- **Plant / food-based enzymes:** The two best-known food-based enzymes are papain (papaya) and bromelain (pineapple) but all raw foods are rich in enzymes.

- **Animal-sourced enzymes:** In the medical world, manufacturers have been able to extract pancreatic enzymes containing a blend of protease, lipase and amylase from the pancreas of both bovine (cow) and porcine (pig) sources. In the supplement world you will see pancreatic enzyme listed as pancreatin and then the concentration denoted with 4x, 8x or higher, with a higher concentration number indicating a higher potency in that supplement.

- **Fungal-based enzymes:** Derived from various strains of aspergillus, sourced from mushrooms, these fungal-based enzymes make a great choice for vegetarians. Protease, lipase and amylase can all be made by fungal sources.

**TAKE HOME POINT:** Degenerative conditions are the pressing health concern of our times. While degenerative conditions are common they do not have to be a part of your aging process. The single greatest action you can take to maintain an optimal level of health is to keep your enzyme levels high. Doing so means eating more raw foods which are high in enzymes.

If you experience the post-lunch coma, bloating, gas, constipation or abdominal irregularity, simply take a full spectrum digestive enzyme supplement with your meals for 30 days. If you are living with insufficient enzymes, the difference will feel like a miracle. Long term use of digestive enzymes may be a huge benefit, so please consult your physician and ask if long term use is ok for you.

## 4 Keys to Understanding Enzymes

1. Enzyme names frequently include both a prefix and suffix describing the specific enzyme. The prefix represents the substrate (specific food type) the enzymes will react with and the suffix –ase indicates it is an enzyme. Ex. Amylase: Amy (for starch) and –ase (for enzyme).

2. Enzymes only attach to a specific substrate by what is called a "Lock and Key" formation. For example, amylase (the key) can only attach to specific types of starch (the lock) as both the size and shape are specific to each other. Other examples include lipase, which can only attach to fats, and proteases, which can only attach to specific proteins.

3. Individual enzymes remain inactive in the body until they enter the specific environment or location in the digestive tract where both the pH and temperature activate, or "turn on," that specific type of enzyme. This aspect predominantly affects proteases where you will find their names indicate what pH they work in. For example, protease 4.5 will activate in a pH of 4.5, neutral protease in a neutral pH, etc.

4. Quality enzyme supplements list enzymes on the supplement facts label as "units of activity" rather than weight alone (such as milligrams). That's because weight is not a good indicator of enzyme effectiveness and enzymes will vary in concentration and weight. For example, there can be two similar capsules of the same weight (mg) of one enzyme. Of those two, one may have a higher concentration and the other a lower concentration. The lower concentrated enzyme will work far less effectively than the same weight of the higher concentrate enzyme. You won't know this by comparing enzymes by weight alone.

## Digestive Enzymes

Let's now take a look at most of the enzymes that break down carbohydrates, fats and proteins. The chart we've created shows the individual enzymes, unit of measure, range of dosing per one capsule if you were looking at a supplement fact box for a digestive enzyme product, and the action of the enzyme.

- The number of enzymes that break down carbohydrates, starchy fiber and sugars is long and highly specific to different parts of the plant or milk sugar in the case of lactase. If you eat a diet rich in fruits and vegetables, look for a product with activity levels toward the high end of the displayed range.

- Proteolytic enzymes work in a complex fashion to perform digestion, so I will try to explain their role in basic terms. Proteolytic enzymes break down protein bonds in two different ways: one group breaks down larger chunks of proteins into smaller bits of proteins while the others break down those smaller protein bits into the individual amino acids used by your body.

Proteolytic enzymes also fall into the category of metabolic enzymes. You may also hear them referred to by the term systemic proteolytic enzymes. These are the same enzymes that break down the protein in the steak you had for dinner. They are referred to as systemic when they perform the work of breaking down proteins such as fibrin (scar tissue) outside of the gut.

- Lipase is the one enzyme that breaks down fat. While sugars and proteins need many different types of enzymes, lipase relies on bile to first emulsify the fat into smaller units. Then the lipase breaks down these triglycerides into fatty acids which can be used by your body for energy.

But wait, that's not the end of the lipase story. Remember we wrote this book in order for you to learn about foods and how food can heal your body. What I'm about to tell you, in my opinion, is one of the most important aspects of this book:

*We all need to have optimal production of both bile and lipase in order for our cells to work hard enough to heal our bodies from whatever current condition we are in.*

Here is the key, our cells have an outer wall called the cell membrane. That membrane is made up of both fat and embedded proteins. For cell membranes to maintain an optimal level of cell permeability, your body needs optimal fat digestion to ensure cell membrane can do its job. You see, it's the cell membrane that allows for optimal insulin metabolism as well the movement of nutrients in through the cell wall and metabolic waste out. That is how we heal.

The following chart lists many of the enzymes that are currently available in supplement form. You'll likely never see a supplement with all of these enzymes in one product, nor would all of them hit the high end of the enzymes activity level range. Instead, this chart simply offers a picture of the many enzymes now commercially available.

One last caveat, as discussed above, enzyme products you find on the market may use different "units of measure." Some enzymes manufacturers simply use different units of measure to ensure their enzymes are not comparable, and thus appear unique. In the chart on the following page we use the most common units of measure for each enzyme.

| Enzyme | Unit of Measure | Dosing Range per Meal | Action of the Enzymes |
|---|---|---|---|
| **Carbohydrate** | | | |
| Amylase | DU | 5000–20000 DU | breaks down starches into glucose |
| Lactase | ALU | 250–900 ALU | breaks down lactose (milk sugars) |
| Invertase | SU | 350–675 SU | breaks down sucrose into glucose |
| Alpha-galactosidase | GaLU | 150–350 GaLU | break down beans, legumes, seeds, soy |
| Malt Diastase | DP | 100–300 DP | breaks down polysaccharides |
| **Starchy Fiber** | | | |
| Pectinase | endo-PG | 10–20 endo-PG | breaks down pectin (found in berries) |
| Xylanase | XU | 150–250 XU | breaks down xylan (found in wheat) |
| Cellulase | CU | 500 CU | breaks down cellulose into glucose |
| Hemicellulase | CHU | 1000–2500 CHU | breaks down cell walls (hemicellulose) |
| Phytase | FTU | 10–20 FTU | separates phosphate and other minerals from phytic acid found in plant-based foods |
| Beta-Glucoamylase | BGU | 10–50 BGU | breaks down starch to glucose |
| **Fat** | | | |
| Lipase | FIP | 1300–7500 FIP | breaks down fats into fatty acids |
| **Protein** | | | |
| Bromelain | FCCPU | 40,000–100,000 FCCPU | breaks down proteins, anti-inflammatory |
| Papain | FCCPU | 40,000–100,000 FCCPU | breaks down proteins, anti-inflammatory |
| Trypsin | USP | 20,000 USP | breaks down proteins |
| Chymotrypsin | USP | 3,333 UsP | breaks down proteins |
| Peptidase | DPPIV | 10–50 DPPIV | breaks down proteins to amino acids |
| Pepsin | SAPU | 200 SAPU | breaks down proteins, at different pH levels |
| Protease SP | HUT | 25,000–100,000 HUT | breaks down proteins, at different pH levels |
| Protease S | PC | 2500–10,000 PC | breaks down proteins, at different pH levels |
| Protease 4.5 | HUT | 50,000–75,000 HUT | breaks down proteins, at different pH levels |
| Acid Stable Protease | SAPU | 250–400 SAPU | breaks down proteins, at different pH levels |
| Neutral Protease | PC | 2000 PC | breaks down proteins, at different pH levels |
| **Blended** | | | |
| Pancreatin 4x, 8x,10x | USP | Concentration dependent | Contains Protease, Lipase and Amylase |

## Other Digestive Aids

Here are some additional digestive aids important for proper digestion, absorption and utilization of the nutrients, and elimination of waste.

### Bile

Bile contains bile acids crucial for digestion and absorption of fats and fat-soluble vitamins like A, D, E and K. Bile is secreted by the liver and your gallbladder should be full of it.

If you begin to notice a consistent difference or change in your stool (pale in color, constipation or diarrhea) it could be that your liver is not producing enough bile or that your bile ducts are not letting the bile drain properly. Be aware some drugs like NSAIDs, birth control pills, and certain antibiotics can cause drug-induced hepatitis or inflamed liver. If you have any concerns in this area, please see your physician sooner rather than later.

Digestive aid supplements with bile typically range from 50mg to 500mg with 45% cholic acid. The specific dose you use should be determined in consultation with your physician.

Fun Fact: If you eat a piece of chocolate, in about two minutes you will hear your gallbladder squirt out the needed bile to break down the fat in the chocolate. So don't eat chocolate if you plan to sit in a quiet room; others will hear your stomach talking to you!

### Prebiotics and Probiotics

Prebiotics and probiotics as digestive aids are often paired together as they work in tandem.

Prebiotics are nondigestible sugars and starches that become the nutrients needed for probiotics to flourish. The two most common prebiotics are inulin fiber and fructooligosaccharides (FOS).

Probiotics on the other hand are many different strains of beneficial bacteria which work in the small intestine to primarily support our immune systems. They also help in the fermentation of indigestible carbohydrates and break down lactose.

Here is the really important part: as a result of the fermentation process these probiotics produce lactic acid, which plays a crucial part in the digestive cycle. Lactic acid triggers the pancreas and gallbladder to release the needed enzymes and bile we talked about earlier.

## Fiber

This chapter would simply be incomplete without talking about fiber. Fiber comes from the portion of fruits and vegetables your body does not absorb as nutrients. It is the roughage that passes through your stomach, small intestine and colon and out of your body. Fiber helps lower blood cholesterol and reduces constipation.

Ideally, men should get 30 to 38 grams of fiber per day and women should get 21 to 25 grams of fiber per day. Dietary fiber obtained through fruits and vegetables is the best way to get fiber, it may be difficult to get as much as you need through diet alone. Supplementation is a great, cost effective way to boost your daily fiber intake. In proper amounts, fiber supplements can safely be taken daily and used long term. Laxatives, however, should be used only short term to help regulate your system.

If you are insufficient in fiber, take your time to increase your fiber intake. Adding too much fiber at once can cause bloating and stomach cramps. Adding fiber gradually will give the healthy bacteria in your digestive system the opportunity to adjust to the change without causing unnecessary pain and suffering. It's also important to stay hydrated, as water helps the fiber work its way through your digestive system better.

### KEY POINTS:

- An imbalance somewhere is an imbalance everywhere.
- Enzymes, fiber, digestion, absorption of nutrients and the role of supplements all play a part in helping you restore balance in your body.

# Busting the Myth Behind Fad Diets

There is a logical reason why you feel unwell. If you find yourself frequently sick, lethargic or run down with general malaise, look to your diet as a root cause. The foods you eat, how much you eat and when you eat all affect your total health picture.

Many look to fad diets when trying to make a change and take first steps toward a healthier diet. While we are not going to pick sides, support or defend any certain type of fad diet, we want to educate you to make sure you know how and why certain foods (not diets) will help you get out of pain.

The ultimate goal with any dietary change is to make food your friend. Whether you grow it or or buy it from the store, what we find always works best is to understand the pros and cons, including what different foods and food plans are best for your body rather than blindly following a fad plan.

The two most important things to consider for healthy eating do not involve fad diets. Instead, consider:

1.  How many total calories you take in.

2.  How to maintain a balance of specific nutritional needs based on your current situation and the course of your entire life.

## A Brief History of Fad Diets

Rather than tell you to *never* try fad diets we wish to help you understand how what you choose to eat should be specific to your individual circumstances as opposed to blindly following a diet system that is "proven" to work.

There are personalized circumstances that no single diet can answer. We want to help you educate yourself so you can make your own decisions about food: what to eat, how much to eat and when to eat it. Ultimately, the plan you create should help you control the inflammatory response occurring in your body, reduce your pain, increase your ability to be functionally mobile and operate at a higher level of optimal health.

Fad diets are creative and they are not all bad. Our main concern with fad diets is they typically do not educate, inspire and empower you to make your own informed decisions about your health. Fad diets are commonly centered around weight loss, which is a great goal. However, failing to take a holistic approach means some of these weight loss fad diets set you up for failure.

Let's take a look at some of the most popular fad diets over the years:

1930s:
- The Hollywood Diet (the grapefruit diet): Promises that eating a grapefruit with each meal will help you slim down.

1950s:
- The Cabbage Soup Diet: Promises weight loss of 10 to 15 pounds per week by limiting your diet to cabbage soup.
- The Tapeworm Diet: promises you will lose weight by eating a pill filled with tapeworms.

1963:
- Weight Watchers: Asks you to pay for their program and food, promising weight loss.

1970s:
- Feingold Diet: Geared toward people with ADHD, on the autism spectrum or with other childhood emotional disturbances, this diet's primary objective is to help parents make better food choices free of chemicals.

1975
- Mediterranean Diet: Inspired by the dietary patterns of Greece, Southern Italy, and Spain in the 1940s and 1950s, this diet promises to lower heart disease. The idea is that this type of diet *over a lifetime,* can improve the quality of life *over your entire life span.*

1977:
- Slim Fast: Promises weight loss through their program of a shake for breakfast, a shake for lunch and a sensible dinner.

1985:
- Fit For Life: Harvey and Marilyn Diamond promise weight loss with a diet where complex carbs and protein cannot be eaten during the same meal.

1992:
- Atkins Diet: Promises a high-protein, low-carb plan is the key to weight loss.

1995
- The Zone Diet: Promises a specific ratio of carbs, fat and protein at each meal is the key to weight loss.

2003
- The South Beach Diet: Considered a moderate version of Atkins with the same promise of slimming down with their plan.

2011
- HCG Diet: Combines a fertility drug with a strict 500- to 800-calorie-a-day regimen.

2013
- Dash Diet: Was developed to help lower blood pressure without medication in research sponsored by the US National Institutes of Health.

## Weight Loss

Presumably anyone reading this book wants to be healthy and fit. Many are also in a position where they would like to lose weight. Weight loss as part of a healing plan is a great option, as being overweight promotes systemic inflammation.

When attempting to lose weight, you will want to consider both your total caloric intake and your daily nutritional requirements. Not everyone in pain will need to lose weight; take your personal situation into consideration and ask yourself what actions you should take to bring yourself back into balance, one step at at time. Whether weight loss is part of your goal to get out of pain or not, we encourage you to make healthy choices and eat in a optimal manner.

## Vegetarian Diets

We do not consider vegetarian diets to be fad diets. If you are new to a vegetarian diet, please take the time to review your intake to ensure you get the full spectrum of proteins, fats, vitamins and minerals your body requires.

Also understand that when you are in a healing crisis, a strictly vegetarian diet can be nutritionally limiting. If you find yourself in chronic pain or a degenerative state, consider adding proper supplementation to provide any missing nutrients you may not be getting through your diet.

## KEY POINTS:

- Eating in excess or deficiency as many fad diets call for can be detrimental in the long term: balance of daily caloric intake matters when resolving health detriments.

- With regard to fad diets: educate yourself to all the variables, pros and cons specific to what you want to do with your health and make diet choices accordingly.

- You will eat every day for the rest of your life. Changing your meal plans and eating habits is a tool you can implement right away to help yourself on a daily basis. Take this book as a first step in understanding food, meal plans and nutritional requirements.

- Inflammation can be caused by the types of food you eat and the total quantity of foods you eat. Do not lean on fad diets to get you out of an inflamed state.

- Feeling better has much to do with monitoring what you eat and how much you eat: eat non-inflammatory foods while you are healing and getting out of pain.

- Ultimately, you hold the responsibility for learning about responsible eating, diet or exercise. Let us educate and equip you with some tools and inspire you to make your own food- and diet-related decisions from an empowered place.

# CREATIVE COOKING WITH
# HERBS, SPICES AND CONDIMENTS

Condiments, herbs and spices are your secret weapon in the kitchen. They not only add flavor, but are nutritionally beneficial. They give any meal a distinct taste, which can encourage someone to cook a dish more frequently if it's both appetizing and healthy.

Herbs and spices supply the most nutrients when used freshly picked or shortly after they are dried. The spice container of dried basil that has sat in your pantry for a year does not provide the same medicinal properties as freshly picked basil. Most spice companies suggest tossing the spice after a year of shelf life. One idea to avoid wasting spices (and money on spices you might not want to have a lot of) is to buy them just a few ounces at a time from the bulk containers in your local grocery store. If you are buying from the bulk containers, keep an eye out for mold and avoid purchasing moldy spices.

If you have tried a new herb or spice and after multiple uses still don't like the taste, there are other ways you can still benefit from your purchase rather than letting it go to waste. Some ideas: you can make a tea, poultice, or use it in your bath. Dry and burn it as incense. Make a healthy tincture out of it.

## Salt and Pepper

The most common additions to our foods are salt and pepper. You can think of these seasonings as having medicinal value and use them accordingly.

There is a difference between sea salt and common table salt. Sea salt is comprised of many beneficial electrolytes, minerals and ions, but lacks iodine (commonly added to table salt as an supplemental additive). If you use sea salt, remember you may need to obtain iodine from other sources such as fish. This is important because without enough iodine your thyroid cannot function properly. Himalayan, Kosher and Celtic Salts are all preferable options to table salt, but we advise you choose Sea Salt with the understanding you will likely need to get iodine through other food sources. Also be sure to source your sea salt from the best possible waters. It is counterproductive to eat sea salt from toxic waters.

Pepper comes from the fruit of the peppercorn plant, which is dried and ground into the pepper we add to food. Peppercorn is known to have antibacterial properties, helping relieve cold symptoms, constipation and indigestion. It is an anti-inflammatory and assists the digestive process. It contains manganese, iron, potassium, vitamin C and vitamin K.

Of course, if you use salt and pepper in excess and create an imbalance in your system, either of these spices can yield negative effects over time. While small amounts of salt are beneficial for your health, certain people will not be able to tolerate salt if they are in an extreme imbalance (such as those with high blood pressure). And while pepper in small amounts is great for you, too much pepper can cause irritation. Again, the message with using salt and pepper is the same as the message echoed throughout this book: use them in balance, as medicine.

## Herbs That Fight Inflammation and Ideas to Use Them in Cooking

### Cloves
- Spike an onion with cloves and put it in a crock pot to stew with a roast.
- Spike an apple or orange with cloves when making mulled hot drinks.
- Spike a ham with cloves, drizzle with honey and bake accordingly until done.

### Cinnamon
- Add cinnamon to your hot beverages (teas, coffees, mulled drinks).
- Sprinkle cinnamon on butternut squash then add walnuts, a little butter or oil and bake.
- Bake apple and fennel cubes with a sprinkle of cinnamon and dot of butter.

### Jamaican Allspice
- Baked Jamaican jerk chicken skewers.
- Add to meatloaf for an exotic twist on an old favorite.
- Add to barbecue sauces.

### Oregano
- Make an anti-inflammatory vinaigrette with oregano, lime or lemon, garlic, salt and olive oil.
- Bake chicken, shrimp or fish with a Mediterranean blend of oregano, olives, garlic, lemon, onion, salt and pepper. Make it vegetarian by using the blend on potatoes or asparagus instead of meat.

- Homemade tomato sauce with fresh oregano is a surefire winner if you include nightshades in your diet.

### Marjoram

- Bake chicken, shrimp or fish with tangerines or orange circles and marjoram.
- Leafy green salad with beets, marjoram, sesame seeds and an orange vinaigrette.
- Sauté root vegetables (carrots, potatoes, etc.) and coat with a lemon and marjoram dressing.
- Use it in your favorite healthy Italian recipe.

### Sage

- Use it in lamb burger patties.
- Make a white bean hummus with sage.
- Use it with butter on baked fish or squash.

### Cayenne

- Use on blackened chicken or fish.
- Use it on any Cajun-themed meal.
- Use it in chicken tortilla soup.
- Use it in chili.

## Hot Peppers

Hot peppers contain anti-inflammatory capsaicin and are an appetite suppressant. They're nutritionally beneficial as they contain vitamins A and C. However, be aware they're also part of the nightshade family which may contribute to your pain as discussed in The Complete Healing Formula™ Applied to Nutrition chapter.

## Condiments

Condiments are a non-traditional area to consider when seeking to add nutrition to your diet. Depending on which you choose, condiments can either help or hurt you. Be sure to select organic products with no added sugars, no food coloring and limited preservatives when possible. Because sugars and additives increase inflammation, they should be avoided while getting out of pain and into a more balanced state of health.

### Mustard

Mustard seeds and leaves are full of healing properties. As a condiment we are focusing on the mustard seed, which is used to make the table mustard common in household refrigerators. Mustard seeds contain several beneficial minerals such as calcium, magnesium, phosphorus and potassium. They also contain vitamin A and dietary folate.

Let's review the various types of mustards. While various brands will have different recipes and properties, here's a bird's eye view of mustard varieties:

- Yellow Mustard: mustard seed and turmeric usually give this spread it's bright color and are mixed with vinegar and water to create the final product. However, basic yellow mustard sometimes contains food coloring. Look for brands that do not contain any artificial coloring or flavors.

- Honey Mustard: usually a 1:1 ratio of honey and mustard. Watch for added sugars.

- Brown Mustard: this concoction is made by soaking brown mustard seeds in less vinegar than the yellow mustard. It is more coarse in texture and great on deli sandwiches.

- Dijon Mustard: a grape juice blend is used instead of vinegar, making this mustard less acidic than others.

- Whole Grain Mustard: typically uses a white wine instead of vinegar, although specialty mustards use various forms of red wines.

In addition to eating mustard, you can make a poultice out of the seeds or powder and apply to muscle aches and pains. Be careful and seek proper instruction if trying this at home as mustard has properties that may burn if applied improperly.

## Ketchup

Ketchup is made from tomatoes and seasonings. It's a great way to add flavor without adding unnecessary fat, carbohydrates or calories. One nutritional benefit ketchup offers is lycopene, an antioxidant present in cooked tomatoes. It also tends to be a source of vitamin A.

Unless you're making ketchup from scratch, there are a few things to take into consideration. Like anything processed and store bought, we encourage you to read the nutritional label and watch out for high sugar content–especially from high fructose corn syrup. Sugar is the number one cause of inflammation, which you will want to avoid while trying to get out and stay out of pain.

## Vinegar

Vinegar is used in dressings, mustards, marinades and sauces and used for pickling and preserving food. You can make flavored vinegars or herbed vinegars by adding your favorite fruits and spices. Vinegars go through a process of fermentation, some slow and some more lengthy.

White vinegar is made from grains, while apple cider vinegar is made from apples. If you are avoiding grains to help reduce inflammation, stay away from distilled (white) vinegar. Apple cider vinegar is a healthier choice. It contains more trace vitamins and minerals than white vinegar. Make sure you find one that is organic, unfiltered and raw.

Apple cider vinegar is antibacterial and anti-inflammatory. Some use vinegar as a natural cleaning product in their home for mopping or cleaning mirrors and windows. Others use it as a beauty product to clean their face, cleanse the hair or even whiten teeth. It can also be used as a weed killer and odor neutralizer.

To incorporate this helpful 'condiment' in your daily diet, add a tablespoon of apple cider vinegar to your water bottle and drink it throughout the day. Add a little honey if the taste is too bitter when you first start drinking it. Use balance and caution to avoid drinking too much, as apple cider vinegar is highly acidic.

## KEY POINTS:

- Condiments, herbs and spices can be used to add more medicinal value to your food.
- Good news: Peppers with capsaicin and mustards are antibacterial and anti-inflammatory.
- Ketchup adds flavor without adding unnecessary fat, carbohydrates or calories. Be sure to get an organic brand that is not loaded with sugar.
- If you are using vinegar in cooking or with your daily water, choose a raw, organic and unfiltered apple cider vinegar.

# EXPLORE ALTERNATIVE COOKING TECHNIQUES & KITCHEN GEAR

The temperature at which you cook your food and the equipment you use to cook and store your food play a role in your health. If you use pots and pans with heavy metals that leech into your food, you are adding toxic chemicals into your diet. Similarly, if you store food in containers that contain toxic chemicals, you are harming your food.

Over time, toxic metals contribute to a long list of maladies including neurological disorders, Parkinson's disease and Alzheimer's. Acute metal toxicity includes symptoms from sweating and vomiting to impaired neurological function. Buildup of toxic chemicals in your body can cause fatigue, depression, digestive disorders, joint pain and more.

It's best to avoid toxic chemicals whenever possible, so we suggest you avoid cooking with equipment that may leach heavy metals into your food supply. In this chapter we will discuss best practices with cooking equipment and food storage as well as considerations for cooking temperatures and pros and cons of microwaving all of which affect your overall health.

## Cooking Equipment to Avoid

### Stainless Steel

- Stainless steel is a steel alloy made primarily from iron but it also contains toxic chromium and toxic nickel. Research has found that all three of these metals leach into both acidic and alkaline foods and beverages, but they do not leach into water. Even a simple task like spreading peanut butter with a stainless steel knife has shown the nickel forms a film and slides into the food. It simply is not worth it when there are other options.

- Reduce the amount of food you eat at restaurants, as many of them are required to store food in stainless steel.

- Some food products such as several forms of soy are processed through stainless steel machines. This is one of the many reasons it is always better to eat whole foods than processed foods.
- To further eliminate stainless steel from your daily routine, avoid stainless steel thermoses, stainless steel orthodontics (braces) and certain jewelry.

## Aluminum or Anodized Aluminum

- Using aluminum pots and pans adds aluminum to your food. In excess, aluminum is toxic. The longer food sits in an aluminum pan, the more aluminum is absorbed into the food. Acidic foods such as tomatoes absorb the most aluminum.
- Older aluminum cookware should be discarded completely as more aluminum is leached from them while cooking.
- To further eliminate aluminum from your daily routine, avoid cosmetics and deodorants that contain aluminum.
- We do not advise using aluminum foil in food storage or cooking.

## Copper

- Similar to aluminum, copper is a toxic heavy metal when ingested in excess. Although it is an excellent conductor of heat, it can leach toxic amounts of copper into your food, even when the pan is coated in another substance. When copper builds up in the body without detoxifying properly, it can cause chronic illness.

## Teflon / Non-stick

- Teflon is a manmade chemical. When used at high heat, or when particles break off during cooking, teflon emits harmful substances that can irritate and hurt people and pets.

## Safer Cooking Equipment Alternatives

### Glass

- Cooking with glassware such as Pyrex is a good option because glass does not absorb odor or flavor, nor does it react with the foods you are cooking. You can store leftovers in the same container you bake in, making clean up that much easier.

### Cast Iron

- Safe to use both in the oven and on the stovetop, cast iron is a safe option for cooking. These pans can leach iron into the food you are cooking, but not at toxic levels. Because the body does not eliminate iron naturally (unless donating blood or through regular menstruation), there is the rare chance that iron buildup could accumulate to toxic levels in some individuals. Season the pan according to brand instructions and do not wash with soap but rather follow each brand's instructions.

## Enamel Coated Cast Iron

- Similar to cast iron, except these pans do not add extra iron to your food. In cheaper brands, enamel may chip off which makes the food unsafe. Do not use metal utensils to stir or cook within an enamel coated cast iron pan as it will scratch the surface and make it unsafe to cook with.

## Titanium

- Premium titanium cookware does not react with food and does not pose health risks.

## Stoneware and baking stones

- Stoneware and most baking stones are made with natural, nontoxic clay, which does not harm the body.
- Season the pan according to brand instructions and do not wash with soap but rather follow each brand's instructions.

## Ceramic

- Ceramic cookware is nontoxic and does not react with foods while they are cooking. They do not require special seasoning nor are they affected by the type of utensil used to cook with them. Beware of low quality ceramics that may contain toxic lead which can leach into the food. Ceramic crock pots are preferable to enamel crock pots because enamel crock pots may leach lead into food when used at high heat.

## Corningware

- CorningWare® is bakeware made from glass-ceramic material that can be used both in the oven and on the stove. It's also a safe container for food storage, making it easy to store leftovers in CorningWare® in the refrigerator then take it straight to the oven to reheat without creating additional dirty dishes. Note: the original CorningWare® was manufactured by Corning Glass Works beginning in 1958. CorningWare® and Corelle® are now both owned by World Kitchen which relaunched the brand in 2001.

# Utensils

There are several options regarding utensils to eat, cook and serve with on the market. These include silver, stainless steel, bone, shell, wood, bamboo, copper, plastic, silicone and more. The more natural the utensil, the better. The main thing to remember with many utensils is you expose your system to heavy metals or toxic chemicals every time you touch them. In addition to playing it safe with your cookware and utensils, you may want to begin a regular detoxification program (see the Cleansing and Detoxing chapter).

## Wood and Bamboo

The primary concern with using wood or bamboo in cutting boards, spoons or food storage is their porosity. Because they are highly porous, bacteria or chemicals from food can easily get lodged in the surface. When using wood, bamboo or any other highly porous material in cooking, be sure to clean the equipment thoroughly before and after each use. To sanitize a wooden cutting board you can use a solution of one tablespoon of unscented, liquid chlorine bleach per gallon of water. Any cutting board, spoon or storage container with large grooves should be discarded.

## Sponges

Kitchen sponges used in cleaning harmful bacteria can grow yeasts, germs and molds if not cleaned properly. To sanitize your sponges, microwave them on high for one minute or put them through a dishwasher cycle with a water temperature of 140 °F (60 °C) or higher. Failure to sanitize sponges allows them to spread harmful germs to your kitchen and food supply.

## Proper Food Storage

Proper food storage is another area where you can help or hurt your health. There are several benefits to storing leftovers: you save money by stretching the food over the course of a few days, they have a 3- to 5-day shelf life, you can repurpose the food into another dish, etc. But if you store your food in a plastic container and reheat it in that same container, you both damage the food and decrease your optimal level of health for that day.

Chemicals in plastic leach into food, especially in extreme temperatures such as freezing and high heat. Plastic storage containers made with Bisphenol A (BPA) leach this industrial toxic chemical into your food. While putting room temperature food into room temperature plastic seems to pose less risk of BPA exposure, we advise you to never put hot food into plastic or heat food while in plastic. We also do not advise using aluminum foil in food storage or cooking. Use parchment paper as an alternative when possible.

Glass bowls with tops are the best choice for food storage.

## Cooking Temperatures

The most nutritious your food will ever be is in its raw state at the peak of ripeness. The longer it remains off the vine, the less nutrients it will have. Flash freezing fruit or vegetables in their peak ripeness is a great way to maintain nutrients. Dehydrating or canning foods is another way to preserve fresh food, but it does not preserve the full value of the original nutrient content.

Cooking reduces nutritional content. The higher temperature you use, the less nutrients your food will retain.

Advanced glycation end products (AGEs) are proteins or lipids that become bonded to sugar molecules without the help of enzymes. Formed primarily through charring meat, or cooking meats at extremely high temperatures, AGEs are considered a factor in several degenerative and chronic diseases.

- Cooking your meat slowly at a lower temperature produces a healthier meat. Be sure to cook all meat to the appropriate temperature to kill bacteria and pathogens.

- 160 °F to 175 °F (71 °C to 79 °C) is an ideal internal temperature for poultry, beef, lamb and pork.

- Chicken should never have any pink on the inside, though some prefer to eat beef or pork more rare. In those cases, the United States Department of Agriculture claims it is ok to cook as low as 140 °F (60 °C).

- A good rule of thumb is to use an internal thermometer when you cook meat to ensure you have reached a safe internal temperature and that the meat is thoroughly cooked but not singed.

Microwaving has been a controversial issue for several years. We acknowledge microwaving is a common form of modern cooking, but we caution you to use it in moderation due to harmful EMF rays microwaves emit while in use. If you have the time to heat your food on the stove or oven in proper cookware, that is the healthiest choice.

# WARNING: FOODS TO AVOID

## Foods to Avoid at All Times

Food is not just something our bodies receive and enjoy. Rather, food contains micronutrient-information for our bodies to decode and work with to fuel or heal our cells. Food is either healing or hurting you. No matter what type of diet strategy you implement, there are certain foods everyone should avoid or limit. Sugar, artificial sweeteners and high fructose corn syrup have no nutritional value. Neither do processed meats, food dyes and trans fats. Supplemental facts labels only provide a partial picture of what's inside so be sure to review the ingredients list as well. Stay informed about what you put in your body because your body will try to use what you give it for fuel and healing.

Here are a few suggestions of foods we should all **avoid**:

Sugar, artificial sweeteners and high fructose corn syrup
- Processed sugars are the worst thing you can put into your body if you are trying to reduce inflammation.
- Examples of processed sugars include sodas, candies and packaged sweets.

Processed meats
- Much of the calorie content in processed meats comes from fats. Eating processed meats regularly is a poor choice for long term optimal health.
- Examples of processed meats: certain hot dogs, lunch meats, etc.

Food dyes
- Artificial coloring is made from toxic, synthetic ingredients that have adverse effects on health. It is best to omit these from your diet.
- Read food labels carefully to avoid artificial coloring such as Yellow 5 and Yellow 6.

Trans fats
- Also known as hydrogenated or partially hydrogenated fats, trans fats are toxic fats that increase levels of bad cholesterol, increases blood clotting and contributes to weight gain.
- Avoid margarine and choose real butter instead.

## Foods to Avoid During Certain Conditions

At times you will need to modify your eating plan. For example, if you are ill with a cold or the flu, your body will use all available energy to fight the illness and return to health so it needs to be fed nourishing food. It is best to avoid meat, wheat, dairy and sugar while you are sick. Instead, choose clear broth soups, steamed vegetables and fresh fruit until you feel better.

Under various weather conditions, you can use food to help regulate your body temperature. It may sound like common sense, but avoid drinking hot drinks and eating hot meals if you are already hot or if it is hot outside. Instead, look for room temperature or chilled drinks and cooler foods such as salads to soothe your body. By contrast, if you are in a cold environment, drinking hot teas and eating warm soups will nourish and warm your body.

If you are overweight or have high blood pressure, it is best to avoid extra fat and calories. Instead, move toward a 2,000 calorie per day diet and choose lean proteins, healthy vegetables and fruits while trying to lose weight.

# Throw Water on the Fire

Beverages are another area we can utilize to improve our health. Teas, tonics and smoothies are supercharged with various nutrients that help cleanse and energize your system. There are small changes you can make with your drinking habits that over time will improve your health, wellness and longevity. For example, drinking tonics and herbal teas with honey have more health benefits and less health risks than a sugary soda.

## How Much Water Should You Drink?

A good goal in water consumption is to drink between 1 to 1.5 ounces per lb of body weight. For example, if you weigh 150 pounds, you'll want to drink 150 to 225 ounces of water per day.

| Weight | = | How Much Water to Drink Daily |
|---|---|---|
| 100 lbs | = | 13 cups |
| 125 lbs | = | 16 cups |
| 150 lbs | = | 19 cups |
| 175 lbs | = | 22 cups |
| 200 lbs | = | 25 cups |
| 225 lbs | = | 28 cups |
| 250 lbs | = | 31 cups |
| 275 lbs | = | 34 cups |
| 300 lbs | = | 37 cups |

A few more suggestions for water intake:

- Drink filtered water.
- Do not drink water from plastic bottles that contain harmful BPAs (bisphenol A), which are toxic chemicals your body will read as an invading contaminant. Plastic bottles that do not contain BPA's will note this on their labeling.

- Drink room temperature water when possible.

While you should stay hydrated by drinking water throughout the day, there are certain considerations in choosing to drink either warm or cold water.

## Benefits of Drinking Warm Water
- Aids in digestion
- Aids in liver detoxification
- Helps clear up nasal congestion
- Challenge: Try drinking a hot drink with your meal and see how you feel.
- Recipe idea: add slices of fresh ginger and honey to hot water to make a stomach-soothing hot water tonic.

## Benefits of Drinking Cold Water
- Regulates body temperature after a workout
- Aids in heat stroke by reducing body temperature
- Boosts metabolism*
- Recipe idea: add some fresh peppermint or lemon and basil to your water to encourage you to drink water more often.

*Note: If you are drinking cold water for weight loss, it is counterproductive to drink cold water while or directly after eating. Cold water inhibits enzymes from activating and assisting with digestion. An example of this is eating a warm hamburger and drinking a cold soda. The coldness of the soda prevents the enzymes from breaking down the food and the food just sits in your stomach.

## Teas 101

Drinking tea is a great way to add nutrition, detox, cleanse or just nourish yourself. Black teas and green teas contain flavonoids, which are known for their antioxidant properties. Adding antioxidants to your daily nutritional intake is a great way to help reduce inflammation and improve overall health.

In addition to black and green teas, which are made from tea leaves, you can make herbal tea from a selection of fresh or dried herbs such as peppermint for an afternoon pick-me-up or chamomile before bedtime to help you relax and wind down.

### Anti-Inflammatory Teas
- Ginger Tea
- Green Tea
- Rooibos Tea
- Rose Hips
- Black Tea
- Willow Bark Tea
- Nettle Leaf Tea

# Easy Meal Planning and "Pain Free" Grocery Shopping

## Meal Planning

Meal planning is the process of making a schedule of what you are going to eat. When meal planning, you will need to carve out some time to pick from the recipes we give you, go to the grocery store or restaurant, and ultimately cook, eat and clean up after each meal. You might want to keep a meal journal or write a specific plan on a calendar that you keep on your refrigerator.

The purpose of meal planning within the context of The Complete Healing Formula™ is to help you take an inventory of what you are eating and help you make balanced choices for grocery shopping and healthy cooking. One main goal with meal planning is to incorporate a variety of foods and nutrition in your eating to reduce inflammation and balance out your diet. Over time, this will be a big factor in getting out and staying out of pain.

For example, if you have chronic nerve pain, but only address this area of pain through chiropractic or physical therapy and do not alter your diet, you may get some pain relief at first. But if you continue to eat a diet rich in inflammatory foods, your body will continue to create an inflammatory response and the pain will eventually return. Food is the only healing solution we must utilize every day for the rest of our lives. We encourage you to look at your pain picture holistically and long term, incorporating balanced food and nutrition into your plan for a healthy life.

If you do not like to cook or rarely cook at home, it may be beneficial to start with a change of perspective to help change your habits. Eating is the one thing we must all do to fuel our bodies on a daily basis. Therefore, it is imperative that we embrace making and eating healthy meals and balanced diets. Removing any mental blocks or cognitive dissonance you may have to planning meals and preparing them at home will increase your willingness and ability to add some great new meal prep habits to your day.

It's ok if you prefer to keep things a little looser with your meal planning. For example, when I go to the grocery store I start in the produce section. Whatever looks fresh and tasty to me at the time is the first thing to go in the shopping cart. If the broccoli looks good, I will put a head or two of broccoli in the cart. From there, I think of my favorite broccoli recipe and make sure to get the remaining ingredients to complete the recipe: garlic, onions, ginger, coconut aminos. Next I think of what protein would go well with that broccoli. My preference is beef, so I head to the meat section and pick up flank steak which I will marinate in the coconut aminos and a little garlic and honey. For me, one dinner meal is complete: I have a protein, a vegetable, and I have added some medicinal roots, herbs and spices along the way. When I get home, I add beef and broccoli to my meal planning list on the refrigerator since that is now an option I have on hand to easily prepare.

Because I have some practice and I know which recipes my household likes the best, as well as which recipes nourish us the most, I am able to develop a recipe in my head based on whatever produce I have put in the cart. But if meal planning is new to you, allow yourself to keep it simple until you get into the habit of regular healthy grocery shopping.

How can you keep meal planning simple? Check out the step by step instructions below.

## Step-By-Step Instructions for Meal Planning

1. Make a short list of healthy proteins, vegetables and fruits that you enjoy.

   - Example: peanut butter, salmon, acorn squash, carrots, strawberries.

2. Find a few recipes for each of them and make a list of possibilities for the week.

   Peanut butter:
   - Banana slices with peanut butter and shredded coconut on top
   - Apple slices with peanut butter spread on top
   - Peanut butter and banana smoothie

   Salmon:
   - Pan-seared salmon with mango chutney and wilted garlic spinach
   - Use the leftover salmon for fish tacos

   Acorn Squash:
   - Baked acorn squash with bacon and pesto
   - Baked acorn squash with walnuts, cinnamon and brown sugar
   - Could get a rotisserie chicken and a pre-made salad mix to go with this

Carrots:

- Carrot sticks and hummus
- Parboiled carrots with herbs
- Shredded carrots, turmeric, raisin salad

Strawberries:

- Berry salad with strawberries, blueberries and raspberries
- Strawberry, basil, balsamic lemonade
- Strawberry, orange juice smoothie

3. Copy or print out the recipes and keep them in a folder in your kitchen.

4. Print your list of possibilities and post it on your refrigerator. You may wish to add a few things that you normally have around the house to give yourself more options. Example: cereal and almond milk, oatmeal with raisins, etc.

5. Determine what you already have on hand at home. Make a grocery list based on what you need and be willing to change the plan a little depending on what is fresh and available at the grocery store.

6. When you get home, put the groceries away. You may wish to give yourself a head start by washing some of the fruits and vegetables or by chopping anything you might need for the next meal you want to cook.

7. As you are making your meals throughout the week, cross them off your list of possibilities you have posted on your refrigerator.

As you form this habit, grocery shopping for specific meal planning will get easier and easier. You can gear your shopping for particular events each week: school lunches, themed entertaining, camping or travel, etc. Make looking for recipes a fun activity by searching through new cookbooks or online sources. Engage the other members of your household to have them help come up with a few recipes they would like to see on your list of possibilities.

## How to Keep Meal Planning Simple

If cooking at home is so overwhelming to you that it is a block to healthy eating habits, take some steps to make it less overwhelming. The mental block is something you can overcome with an open mind, patience and practice.

- Make simple, easy dishes: raw vegetables or fruit do not require much preparation.
- Take a cooking class.
- Watch an online demonstration.

- Invite a friend over to teach you how they make a special dish.
- Participate in a food share: you cook one dish to share with two or three friends and they each do the same. Meet up to trade with everyone and come home with three or four different meals for the week.

Remember why we are encouraging you to engage in meal planning: mapping out your meals will help ensure you get balanced nutrition. This way of planning and eating will help reduce your inflammation and pain because you won't be splurging or waiting to eat until you are past hungry and then make unhealthy choices.

A typical meal planning note (list of possibilities) on my refrigerator will list the food I have for the week broken up into meals or snacks that I like. This way when I am hungry I can see a lot of great ideas to utilize the food I have on hand. Some of the ingredients might be frozen, some might be fresh from the garden and others might be what I bought from the store. When I eat the item on the list, I simply cross it off so I know it is no longer an option.

My current list of possibilities looks something like this:

**Breakfasts:**
Tomato basil crustless quiche

Turkey sausage, wilted breakfast greens and fruit smoothie

Oatmeal with walnuts, apples and cinnamon

Breakfast tacos: potato, bacon, egg & salsa

Raisin bran and rice/almond milk

**Snacks/Lunches:**
Peanut butter and banana slices with chocolate chips

Trail mix

Apple slices with sunbutter

Cashew kale smoothie

**Dinners:**
Meatloaf, mashed potatoes, salad

Bone broth soup, twice baked squash casserole

Pecan crusted chicken, grape salad or beet salad

Teriyaki Salmon with mango salsa and spinach salad

**Desserts:**
Nice cream

Frozen fruit popsicles

Paleo cookies

Coconut power balls

## How to Shop for the Best Foods

The Environmental Working Group is an organization of scientists, researchers and policymakers. They produced two lists based off a report issued by the President's Cancer Panel: "The Dirty Dozen" and "The Clean 15," to help people identify which types of produce should be bought organically and which produce it is ok to be more lenient and purchase conventionally.

The 'clean fifteen' are more acceptable to buy conventionally as they tend to be cleaner, with less toxins and chemicals. However, the "dirty dozen" regularly shows high levels of toxins and chemicals and should only be purchased in organic form. While we maintain it is always best to buy organic whenever possible, review these lists so you can know which foods are always best to buy organic versus those which may be alright to buy conventionally.

### The Clean Fifteen

These foods tend to be cleaner and are acceptable to consume conventionally when organic is not an option.

- onions
- avocados
- sweet corn
- pineapples
- mango
- sweet peas
- asparagus
- kiwi fruit
- cabbage
- eggplant
- cantaloupe
- watermelon
- grapefruit
- sweet potatoes
- sweet onions

### The Dirty Dozen

These conventional foods are extremely high in toxic chemicals such as pesticides. As such, the foods below should only be purchased organically.

- celery
- peaches
- strawberries
- apples
- domestic blueberries
- nectarines
- sweet bell peppers
- spinach, kale and collard greens
- cherries
- potatoes
- imported grapes
- lettuce

### Anti-Inflammatory Grocery Shopping: Produce 101

Grocery shopping is an essential component of a healthy diet. The foods you choose at the grocery store have the ability to set you up for a great healthy week. To keep fresh produce at home, you will want to make about two trips to the grocery store each week.

Once you're more familiar with your favorite recipes and know what is needed for each, the grocery store can become a creative place for you. If you had plans to make broccoli, but the broccoli in the produce section looks old, you'll already have the tools you need to change your plans and make a different choice. If the cauliflower looks like it's in season and there are several healthy options, you could choose cauliflower instead. Then, you can simply think of your favorite cauliflower recipe and get the ingredients to go along with that.

## KEY POINTS:

- It is as simple as this: as you walk through the produce section, select the freshest food that looks the healthiest.

- Most grocery stores offer several anti-inflammatory foods. Below is a guide to help you select the best anti-inflammatory produce available to you. While not comprehensive, it gives you a good overview of how to select certain fruits and vegetables you will want to incorporate into your diet for a pain-free lifestyle.

## Some reminders and quick tips when purchasing and using produce:

- Buy organic when possible.

- Buy locally grown produce when possible.

- Buying organic frozen produce is equally good if not better because the food is picked at its peak nutritional value and flash frozen, which stores their nutrients.

- Cooking frozen food at high temperatures decreases its nutritional value, so use it frozen when possible (such as in smoothies) to get the maximum nutritional benefit.

- Wash all produce with an organic vegetable/fruit cleaning solution when you bring it home.

- Store whole fruit unrefrigerated.

- Store sliced or opened fruit in a glass container refrigerated.

**Apples**
- Buy apples in fall when they are in season.

- Look for crisp, healthy varieties that are not bruised or torn.

- Sliced apples with your choice of nut butter on top makes a great afternoon snack.

- We include a great recipe for green apple slices with tuna salad.

### Avocados

- Buy these very firm with a little give when you lightly squeeze if you want to eat it that day. They ripen quickly, so it is ok to buy these firm and allow them to ripen at home.
- Sliced avocados with a drizzle of honey on top are a unique snack. You can eat them raw, make salsas as in our mango and avocado salsa served with Atlantic salmon or even ice creams such as our Avocado, coconut, mint, lime and honey sherbet

### Bananas

- Bananas are a personal preference. If you buy them green, they will be firm and taste tart. If they are starting to yellow, they will be more ripe and taste a little sweeter. Bananas that are starting to brown and most ripe and can still be bought and enjoyed at their ripest stage.
- It is easy to freeze bananas with the peel on to store them in their own container.
- Sliced bananas with your choice of nut butter on top is a great snack before a workout. Check out our banana bar recipes for ideas.

### Broccoli

- When buying broccoli make sure there is no mold on it.
- Look for a healthy firm stalk that has a fresh clean cut. The stalk should not have any splits or mold that indicates it has been on the shelf too long.
- Broccoli is great raw, or see our garlic, ginger broccoli recipe.

### Brussels sprouts

- Buy Brussels sprouts in the winter when they are in peak season.
- Choose firm and heavy Brussels sprouts.
- An easy way to make Brussels sprouts is to wash and halve them, then cook in a pan over medium-high heat with garlic and bacon.

### Cabbage

- Cabbage and iceberg lettuce should be heavy with good water content. They should be tight and taste sweet.
- Cabbages and iceberg lettuces make great side salads.

### Cantaloupe

- Test to see if a cantaloupe is ready by squeezing the bottom of the fruit (opposite end of the stem). It should have a little give to it when you push on it, not hard.
- Cantaloupe is great alone or wrapped with mint and prosciutto.

## Carrots

- Buy carrots when they are firm and crisp. They should not bend or be flexible.
- To restore crispness to carrots, you can stand them in a glass of cold water.
- If you leave them in a glass of water for a long time, their tops will start to grow. Carrot tops are edible and you can use them to make interesting pestos or as part of an earthy salad.
- Shredded raw carrots are a great combination with avocado and beets as in our ABC (avocado, beets and carrots) salad.
- Carrots dipped in our white bean and sun butter hummus also make a good snack.

## Dark berries

- Most dark berries like blueberries and acai will be prepackaged so you won't be able to pick them out individually.
- If buying fresh, look for firm berries.
- Incorporate dark berries into your daily snacks, as part of breakfast or in smoothies.

## Garlic

- Buy garlic when the whole bulb is firm.
- Make sure no black mold is on the bottom of the garlic where the root grows.
- Roast garlic whole with olive oil, salt and pepper or incorporate minced garlic into numerous recipes. This is a great bulb to have on hand at all times when cooking for a pain-free lifestyle.

## Green beans

- Green beans should be crisp and firm to the touch.
- If they are bendable or soft, they are not good; they should snap.
- Steam green beans lightly with raw sliced almonds, organic extra virgin olive oil, salt and pepper.

## Kiwis

- Buy these when they are firm. There should be a little give to the touch.
- Eat kiwis alone or incorporate into a tropical fruit salad with papayas, mango and citrus fruit.

### Leafy greens

- Buy salad greens or leafy greens when they have a high water content in their leaves. The leaves should be strong and firm, not scarred, bruised or wilted in any way.
- Make a raw salad or lightly steam greens with garlic for a healthy side dish. Try eating greens for breakfast in your smoothie or as a side to bacon. We share leafy greens recipes including Kiwi, Cashew, Kale Smoothie, a crustless garden quiche and Goji turkey breakfast sausage, wilted spinach and pesto eggs.

### Nuts

- Buy nuts raw and avoid any nuts that have mold.
- Use them in trail mixes or eat plain.

### Pears

- Buy these when they are firm. There should not be any give to the touch. If bought firm, they will ripen within the next day or two.
- Use pears in a leafy green salad with strawberries, goat cheese and a balsamic vinaigrette or eat them alone with walnuts and honey.

### Pineapple

- Buy pineapple when yellow, not green. The bottom of the fruit should smell sweet.
- Eat pineapple alone or use it in smoothies or fruit salads.

### Potatoes

- Buy potatoes when they are firm with no give. If they give when you squeeze them, they are too old.
- Do not eat potatoes if they have started sprouting.
- Boil potatoes in chicken broth and eat whole or mashed with your favorite healthy toppings.

### Strawberries

- Look for berries where the seeds are more indented: those are freshest.
- Eat whole or incorporate into salads or smoothies.

### Tomatoes

- Buy tomatoes when they are firm and dark in color. They will soften as they ripen. When you slice into them, they should be a healthy colored flesh with no white starchy streaks that taste mealy.
- Eat alone with salt and pepper or incorporate into quiches or salads.

# WHEN TO ASK FOR HELP

## When and How to Work with a Professional

There are times in your life when you will need to work with a health care professional. You may have an awareness that something is wrong but not know where to start addressing the problem. In this case, we invite you to start thinking outside of the box and be proactive about asking your health care professional to run specific tests for you.

Please understand that the type of tests and what is tested for needs to be worked out between you and your medical practitioner, but not every general physician will be open to the kinds of tests you will want to run. You may need to find a doctor who is willing to take a more holistic approach. There are functional medicine physicians, doctors of osteopathic medicine, chiropractors and nutritionists who can help you find the proper testing to uncover the root cause of your specific problem. It can be frustrating if you wish to run a specific test and your doctor does not agree. Fortunately, there are options today that allow you to have some of these tests done on your own. See the References and Resources chapter for names of some home test labs and how you can order tests from them.

It's important to know your baseline health so you are aware when any changes occur and how you can address each change. We suggest you have basic bloodwork done every six to nine months. We'll discuss specific tests we recommend later in this chapter. If you do not know your current health state, you won't know how to best eat and supplement appropriately.

We want you to think about how you can find the root causes of stagnation in your health. Sometimes it can be small things over time that make a huge difference in your overall health and wellness. We want you to look for disruptors in your (1) food, (2) environment and (3) insufficiencies in your diet.

The list below is not comprehensive, but rather it is a way of introducing you to the idea that some of these issues may apply to you and your specific health concerns. If you don't take the initiative to figure it out, you will remain stuck or stagnant.

## Testing

What we are looking for with testing:

- Excess
- Deficiencies
- Imbalances
- Sensitivities
- Trends in your values

The different types of tests:

- Blood
- Urine
- Stool
- Saliva
- Skin

If you continually feel unwell, the reason may be lurking in your food, environment or insufficiencies within your diet. Below are a few things to consider to help you take control of your health and return to a balanced state.

### 1. Disrupters in Our Foods: Testing for Allergies and Sensitivities

Food is our natural medicine and the best place to make changes when you are beginning to heal from pain. It is one of the few things we will do every day for the rest of our lives and it has a huge impact on our health.

You can make instantaneous improvements if you identify any issues you may have with certain foods, additives or chemicals. There are several things to test in regard to food. Here are some considerations to help you get started:

- Test for food sensitivities, and sensitivities to additives/chemicals: www. ALCAT.com.
- Wash food to remove dirt and human residue that could be making you ill.
- Check your food before eating and throw away any food that has mold growing on it.
- Know the difference between a food sensitivity and a food allergy. You could go a long time without having a severe reaction to a certain food, yet be sensitive to it and have an underlying malaise because of it.
- Test for allergies to foods, especially:
  - Gluten
  - Peanut
  - Eggs
  - Shellfish

Note: You'll find links in the References and Resources chapter that show where you can have these tested on your own.

## 2. Disrupters in Our Environment: Testing Air, Water and Home Products

Remember when we said that everything matters? Well, the air you breath, the water you drink and your personal care products can also be a hidden source of irritation that can cause an inflammatory reaction. Here are some simple ideas for you to follow:

- Have your homes water tested: www.ntllabs.com
- Change your air filters regularly.
- Clean the house: remove visible molds such as those that occur in window seals, under faucets and in other damp areas of your home.
- Remove soaps, home cleaners, cosmetics, shampoos, beauty products and deodorants that contain toxic chemicals and look for nontoxic replacements.
- Home testing kits can be found here: www.prolabinc.com

## 3. Specific Imbalances or Insufficiencies

Below are some common areas where insufficiencies can cause long term health problems. This is not a comprehensive list, but should give you more to think about when trying to find the root cause of pain and other health problems. Knowing your baseline health by testing for these imbalances will give you an idea of what you can do to improve your health.

### Hormones

- Imbalances in hormones can wreak havoc on your health and how you feel on a daily and cyclical basis. Ask your physician to test you with a hormone panel. The three main hormones to inquire about are testosterone, estrogen and progesterone. Testing for imbalances is typically conducted with a blood test. If you identify a hormonal imbalance, speak with your physician or natural pharmacist about options for over-the-counter creams or prescribed bioidentical hormones to help you return to a balanced state. Supporting your adrenals through specific herbal tinctures is also a safe way to naturally balance your hormonal regulation.

### Vitamin D3

- Vitamin D3 is available to you naturally by getting it via sunlight on your skin. If you are not in the sun often or you live farther north, you are most likely deficient in Vitamin D3. Your deficiency can be even worse during winter. If you do not have the ability to get sun on your skin in healthy amounts, you most likely need to supplement with vitamin D3.
- Get a blood test to determine your baseline levels and discuss a strategy with your healthcare provider to determine a proper dosage of how much vitamin D3 to add to make up for the deficiency and return to a balanced state.

## Magnesium and Calcium

- Calcium and magnesium work together. For example: Calcium helps muscles to contract, while magnesium encourages them to relax.

- Calcium requires magnesium for the body to be able to absorb it.

- If you are unbalanced with your calcium and magnesium intake, you may display certain symptoms such as muscle cramps, nausea and anxiety. Over time this can create chronic health conditions. Knowing your baseline, getting tested and making a balanced plan of action to maintain proper levels of magnesium and calcium will help you feel better.

- Foods high in magnesium include nuts such as almonds and cashews, seafood and green vegetables. Foods high in calcium include dark leafy greens, okra, brocolli, cheese and almonds.

- Reduce your intake of sugar and alcohol as these increase magnesium excretion.

- Read The Calcium Lie by Dr. Robert Thomson (available free at www.losethebackpain.com/calcium-lie-gh.php)

## Vitamin B

- B12 deficiencies are very common. Since your body does not make B12, you must get it through your diet and supplementation when necessary. To add B12 to your diet, make sure you eat enough meat, seafood and eggs.

## Dysbiosis

- Also called dysbacteriosis, this is an imbalance in the small intestine with fungal overgrowth that can be caused by overuse of antibiotics, misuse of alcohol, stress or an unbalanced diet.

- If through testing you identify you have dysbiosis, you will need to form a strategy with your healthcare provider to repopulate and balance the bacteria in your gut. In addition to repopulating healthy bacteria through probiotics, you may wish to discuss supplementing extra zinc, curcumin, glutamine and fiber during your rebalancing process.

## Iron

- If you have a deficiency in iron, you are anemic.

- To avoid and/or heal anemia, you can eat in a way that supports optimal level of iron in the blood. Foods rich in iron include red meat, dark leafy greens and dried fruit. An example of an iron rich meal would be a steak and spinach salad. An iron rich snack could be a handful of dried fruit. Remember to always keep balance in your diet: you don't want to eat red meat every day, but it is a great source of iron when you need it to get out of an anemic state.

- You can get minimal amounts of extra iron in your diet by cooking in a cast iron pan.

**Electrolyte imbalance**

- Electrolytes are ions in fluids that transmit electrical impulses for nerve, heart and muscle function. The number of positive and negative ions should be equal. Anything that disrupts this balance can have life-threatening consequences.

- Because there are several electrolytes that perform different functions, having a physician you trust help walk you through a treatment strategy is ideal.

- Using sea salt with your food is beneficial because it provides a healthy balance of electrolytes.

## CICs: A Deeper Look

CICs (Circulating Immune Complexes) are large, undigested proteins that pass from the intestinal tract into the bloodstream. Your body sees them as invaders, thus an immune response is triggered causing inflammation.

Here's what actually happens when CICs run amok:

1. Larger proteins your body cannot fully break down and digest, like gluten, may pass through the small intestine walls (leaky gut) into your bloodstream.

2. Your immune system responds to these proteins (called antigens) by binding them with antibodies. Once bound, these are called immune complexes.

3. These continue to circulate (therefore, a Circulating Immune Complex) in your bloodstream and are deposited in tissue if your body doesn't break them down.

4. Once attached to muscle tissue, a self-sustaining inflammatory cycle can begin as more CICs are generated from the inflamed site, leading to chronic pain and possible tissue damage.

5. Digestive protease enzymes break down proteins in your digestive tract while systemic proteolytic enzymes break down CICs and enable white blood cells to discard the debris. That's another reason both digestive and systemic proteolytic enzyme supplements should be used together as a comprehensive approach to health.

Blood and tissue tests are available to test for CICs. However, the hs-CRP test which measures C-reactive protein inflammation markers may be suitable enough to monitor progress in lowering chronic inflammation for most.

## ACTION STEPS:

1. Find a physician that will listen to you and your requests for testing.

2. Suggest testing for food sensitivities.

3. Consider testing the inside of your home for disruptors like mold.

4. Detox and cleanse through clean eating and supplementation. (See the Cleansing and Detoxing chapter)

5. Take steps to change your mind and the way you look at food and your environment, with an eye to getting better and living at an optimal level of health.

# KICK TOXINS TO THE CURB...

Toxins and chemicals build up in our body over time. Thus, regular detoxing and cleansing is necessary. It is of utmost importance to stay hydrated with clean, filtered water while you are detoxing and cleansing. The water will help purify your system and help with the elimination of toxic build up.

Detoxing can be an uncomfortable process. It does not always feel good while the toxins are leaving your system. It's common to have headaches and feel nauseous. If symptoms persist or worsen, stop your detox and just do a little at a time by cleaning up your diet and eating patterns.

## Detox the Body

- First, stop eating toxic food products.

- Eat clean food and drink filtered water as a way of detoxing.

- Supplements can come second or in conjunction with a healthy diet.

- Many inflammatory infections start in the mouth. Daily use of an all natural mouth rinse such as hydrogen peroxide and seeing your dentist on a regular basis are great ways to detox and maintain oral hygiene.

- Detox the kidneys, liver and colon through food, or through food and supplementation congruently.

- Find a cleansing method that works for you and stick to it.

## Cleansing Methods

The purpose of cleansing is to rid your body of the natural buildup of toxins in our body from contaminants in the food we eat and disruptors in our environment. There are various cleansing methods available on the market today. Similar to fad diets, it is appropriate to be cautious of any cleanses that promise rapid weight loss. If you are in a healing crisis, it may not be the best time to purge and cleanse. Be aware that depending on your state of health, your body may require additional nutrients while healing.

Conversely, you may have considerable toxic buildup and that is the best time to do a cleanse.

## Top-Down Approach to Cleansing

We support Dr. Clark's top down approach to cleansing. In this approach, you start with your mouth, then kidneys, next liver and finally gut. You can reinfect or recontaminate yourself if you don't clean house from the top down. For example, if you are cleansing your gut health first without addressing mouth, kidneys and liver, you can recontaminate yourself as soon as your mouth comes into contact with something harmful. Dr. Clark's website (www.drclark.net) offers a variety of herbal formulas and tinctures that help you cleanse from the top down:

- Mouth
- Kidneys
- Liver
- Gut

## Master Cleanse

The master cleanse is a time honored colon cleanse from 1940 that involves a mixture of lemon, water, cayenne and maple syrup.

## Clay Detox

There are several clay detox formulas available on the market today. Clay will pull toxins from your body.

## Chlorophyll

Known for it's blood purification properties, liquid chlorophyll is a powerful antioxidant. It also reduces swelling, stops candida growth and offers a bioavailable form of iron.

## Herbal blends

Herbal medicine offers a plethora of healing plants that can be made into tinctures, teas and capsules. Because they are in a condensed liquid form, tinctures are the most potent way for your body to receive the plant medicine and allow it to work right away. There are multiple ways herbalists work with plants to convert them into medicine including use of various parts of the plant. Work with your local herbalist to create a formula unique to your conditions.

**Eight herbs that detoxify:**
- Artichoke leaf: pulls heavy metals out while lowering bad cholesterol and high blood sugar.
- Burdock root: purifies blood, cleanses skin, manages free radicals and reduces inflammation. This is a very strong antimicrobial herb to work with that also supports adrenal function.
- Cilantro: pulls heavy metals from the body.

- Dandelion: the whole plant helps you detox, especially stimulating the liver and gallbladder.

- Milk thistle seed: antioxidant that helps liver cells regenerate while reducing inflammation.

- Neem: purifies the blood, removes metabolic waste and is antibacterial, antifungal, antiviral and antiseptic.

- Red clover: purifies blood and breaks down toxins in the lymphatic system (be sure to work with an herbalist on this one to formulate proper amounts).

- Stinging nettle: detoxifies liver and kidneys.

**Three quick herbal detox recipes:**

Always wash and clean herbs and plants thoroughly before ingesting to remove dirt, potential animal waste, mold and environmental toxins.

- Dandelion tea: add the bright yellow leaves to water and simmer 15-25 minutes to add antioxidants and flavonoids to your body. Note: you can also make medicinal dandelion tea from the roasted roots of this plant.

- Cilantro: add ½ cup of the leaves to your smoothies, salads and juices.

- Stinging nettle: steam the leaves and add it to a steamed greens salad. You can also boil the leaves and add them to vegetable broth and other vegetables to make a detox soup. Be careful if you are picking these as the leaves can sting and leave tiny, itchy bumps on your hands. It's better to work with an herbalist while learning to use this plant. You can find this as a tea if you prefer.

## Parasite cleanse

Be aware that killing parasites can be an extremely uncomfortable process. Often both the good and bad bacteria are killed during a parasite cleanse, so you may want to consider repopulating your gut with prebiotics and probiotics after your cleanse has ended and your body has started to heal. Check out the Gut Health chapter for more information on prebiotics and probiotics.

**Parasite killing ingredients:**
- Black Walnut husks
- Cloves
- Wormwood

Note: these must be taken together to kill all stages of parasitic infection from eggs, to larvae to full grown parasite. See Dr. Clark's parasite cleanse at www.drclark.net for a simple yet comprehensive parasite removal program.

**Additional ingredients for parasite cleansing:**

- Ornithine
- Arginine

Note: As parasites die in your system they release toxic ammonia and excessive nitrogren. Orinthine and arginine will assist in the parasite detoxification by helping your body remove these toxins released by the parasites.

## Heavy metal detox

Consider eating a low-fat diet as dietary fat can hold toxins in your body, making it harder to detoxify. Eating a lot of fat while attempting to detox is counterproductive.

Key ingredients to help with heavy metal detoxification:

- Aloe Vera juice: Squeeze out the clear gel-like liquid into juices and smoothies to flush heavy metals out of your system.
- Barley Grass and Spirulina: These plants work together to remove heavy metals from your body.
- Blueberries: Wild blueberries (not cultivated blueberries) harness powerful detoxification properties. They reverse oxidative damage and provide nutritious phytonutrients.
- Seaweed: Specifically, Atlantic dulse is an edible seaweed. Your body will not be affected by any mercury it might contain from being in mercury-contaminated waters as the plant contains the mercury and pulls other toxins from your body as it works its way through your system.

## Castor oil

- Castor oil is a home remedy that has been used for ages to purge and detoxify. The oil is made from Castor seed, which has a unique chemical composition that contains fatty acids. Part of the seed heals and detoxifies, but another part of the seed is deadly if ingested. Castor oil purchased in stores is considered safe by the U.S. Food and Drug Administration as a laxative and purger.
- Speak with your healthcare provider about proper dosage for your condition, but a general rule of thumb is one tablespoon per day for adults and one teaspoon per day for children. You will notice the effects within four to six hours.

## Juice Cleanses

- Selecting quality, organic ingredients is imperative for using juices to cleanse. If you use conventional fruits and vegetables, you will not get the best results.
- Consider doing a juice cleanse one day a week.
- You can juice at home with spinach, celery, cucumbers and apples, or you can buy premade juices from local juice bars.

## KEY POINTS:

- Cleanse consistently. Try cleansing once a week (not once a year).

- If you are fairly toxic, the elimination of toxins can be an uncomfortable process. Drink lots of purified water during a cleanse to help push the toxins out of your system while hydrating your internal organs to help with the detoxification process.

- You can detox today, but you will only stay 'clean' as long as your diet and environment remain clean. In other words, if you do a cleanse and follow it up with poor eating, cooking with toxic utensils, or are living in a moldy environment, your efforts to cleanse will not work well for you.

- Diligently pick brands that use ingredients from pure sources. It would be counter-productive to continue reintroducing the same toxins back into your system.

# Conclusion: Doing the Dishes

For most of us, doing the dishes is the final part of any meal. But it does not have to mean you are done eating for the day as there is always the possibility of another meal, snack, smoothie or even just a glass of water. In much the same way, when we say that "Everything Matters," just like doing the dishes, "Growing and Learning never ends".

Now that you have finished the first half of this book and have a better understanding how insidious imbalances in nutrition can impact our healing, please take into consideration the principles and strategies I have outlined as you move forward with healing. Use these principles in your approach to shopping for food, thinking about food and how you clean, cut and cook your own food. Remember, food is one of the few things all of us will 'do' every day for the rest of our lives. Your thinking and actions in this area will have a huge impact on your health over your lifetime.

Yes, you have many choices. At times the number of choices can feel overwhelming so here is a simple everyday solution: use your gut feeling. When making decisions about food, ask yourself this simple question: is this the best choice of food for me right now? Rely on your gut feeling and stick to your choice. It's ok to simply say "no thank you." If you feel conflicted about the choice in the moment, think about your goals to feel better which will help you stay strong and make the best choices.

Now that you have been empowered to make right choices about food, here's one more piece of advice. Plan for the next 30, 60 or 90 days to NOT tell ANYONE what you are doing in regard to your diet. Simply keep your thoughts and feelings to yourself while you begin to implement these life changes. It has been said that the ones closest to us are our own worst enemies, or put another way, too many cooks in the kitchen spoils the pot.

During Grace, Tiffany touched on how our lives feel controlled by either memories or inspirations and many of us have wonderful memories regarding family gatherings and all the food that was eaten. We want to challenge you to feel inspired. We want to challenge you to do the work that is needed to learn how to cook with these recipes, to get good at them, and at some point, make breakfast lunch or dinner for someone else, and enjoy the feeling of being a good at-home cook.

**THE FINAL TAKE AWAY:** We wrote this book without knowing your current level of knowledge of nutrition or even your cooking ability, so please keep that in mind as you begin to savor and digest The Complete Healing Formula™ driven recipes. It is our hope that you gathered at least a few nuggets of knowledge and that our content and recipes will inspire you to "Make Them Your Own."

# Part 2
# Simple Recipes to Eliminate Pain and Promote Healing

Traditional cookbooks are laid out with appetizers, main courses, side dishes, beverages and desserts. Some cookbooks are organized according to type of food or seasons. Our approach differs slightly in that we acknowledge how our bodies have different nutritional needs throughout the day. Therefore, we organized the recipes according to the time of day so that you can biohack your way to optimal health and healing.

Biohacking is a way to combine your knowledge of your personal body's needs with your knowledge of which foods are best to eat at different times. We offer strategic recipes, but ultimately our hope is that you will continue to educate yourself on your health and tweak the recipes to make them work for you no matter where you are in your healing journey.

# BREAKFAST

Your body has different nutritional needs throughout the day and different nutritional needs while you are healing from pain. Staying properly hydrated will help you maintain fluid levels throughout the day and avoid feeling hungry.

**Easy healthy breakfast recipe ideas:**

- Strawberry banana smoothie
- Peanut butter banana smoothie with cacao
- Migas: scrambled eggs with salsa and tortilla chips
- Breakfast taco bar with your favorite items
- Leftovers for breakfast

Be aware if you have a mental block against an aspect of eating. If you think that making a new recipe is 'hard' then you are setting yourself up for failure before you even try to cook the recipe. Keep an open mind and a positive outlook when experimenting with new ingredients and new recipes that help you maintain a healthy lifestyle.

**Keep coming back to these basic points:**

- Eat the rainbow
- Maintain balance
- Maintain an average caloric intake

We have been taught that breakfast is the most important meal of the day, but why? Skipping breakfast typically does not help you save on calories. At some point, you get hungry and the potential to overeat exists. Over time these mini binge episodes really add up with extra calories. A better choice would be to eat a balanced breakfast to give your body energy to start the day and sustain you for several hours.

**Protein in the morning.**

It's not that protein at night is 'bad' for you, but eating close to bedtime will not be as beneficial because your body needs to shift gears from digestion to sleep. If you balance your protein intake throughout the day by adding some protein to your breakfast, your body has all day to assimilate the protein and make the best use of it. Breakfast sausage, bacon, eggs

and nut butter in smoothies are great sources of protein in the morning. Be sure to pick organic brands when possible.

**Fruit in the morning.**

Fruit is always a good option throughout the day. But if you eat the majority of your fruit at night, it can sit in your stomach and ferment somewhat overnight while the body is not actively digesting. It won't be as beneficial to your health as eating fruit in the morning, either. Fruit smoothies or whole fruit are great options for breakfast.

**Breakfast greens.**

It is common to have leafy greens and vegetables in the evening; if you are eating enough of them that is wonderful. But if you are not getting enough greens in your diet on a daily basis, adding greens in the morning is a great way to incorporate more nutrients into your day. You can cook wilted greens with coconut amino acids, apple cider vinegar, garlic and onions, or you can add spinach or kale (organic, frozen or fresh) to your protein smoothies.

# Goji Turkey Breakfast Sausage, Wilted Spinach and Pesto Eggs

Lean protein in the morning is a great way to kick-start your healing for the day. It fuels muscle recovery and provides energy for your day. It keeps you full, making it easier to avoid binge-eating extra calories when you finally get hungry. As an added bonus, if you need to add a little red (goji and cherries) and green (spinach and pesto) into your day, this recipe will do the trick.

## Goji turkey breakfast sausage

This tasty recipe utilizes superfruit goji berries (also called wolfberries). Native to China, this anti-inflammatory, antioxidant fruit has been eaten for centuries and several Asian cultures claim regular ingestion of Goji increases longevity. Cherries are also a powerful antioxidant and anti-inflammatory.

Makes 3-4 servings.

    1 organic red apple, deseeded and grated

    1-2 tablespoons dried organic goji berries, chopped

    1-2 tablespoons dried organic tart cherries, chopped

    1 pound organic turkey breakfast sausage

    1 tablespoon organic extra virgin olive oil for cooking

Roughly chop the goji berries and cherries and put them in a bowl. Grate the apple and mix in with the berries. Remove any apple seeds that may have fallen in the mix.

Add the turkey breakfast sausage and mix all ingredients besides the olive oil with your hands until everything is incorporated.

Wash your hands and pour a little olive oil into a frying pan. Pat the sausage into small, flat, round patties and cook over medium-high heat for 3-4 minutes on each side or until there is no pink in the middle.

Set cooked patties on a paper towel to drain. Serve warm with wilted spinach and pesto eggs.

### Make It Your Own

- Try rotating different dried fruits and berries as well as different breakfast sausage meats:
- Dried blueberries and apples with pork breakfast sausage
- Dried apricots and prunes with beef breakfast sausage
- Add chopped nuts to increase nutritional value and add a crunchy texture.
- Add different anti-inflammatory spices, like cinnamon, that go well with savory dishes.
- Add a metabolism-boosting dipping sauce like sriracha or cholula.
- Use a different cooking oil of your choosing to add a different flavor element like macadamia nut oil, grapeseed oil or avocado oil.

continued

# WILTED SPINACH

Most of us do not get enough greens in our diet. Adding them to your breakfast routine kick-starts your day with essential nutrition. Spinach is a great choice to always have on hand in your freezer so you always have some nutritious greens available. This recipe utilizes frozen spinach, but you can just as easily swap the frozen spinach for fresh spinach. Frozen spinach has plenty of water without needing to add extra when cooking. If you use fresh, you will want to add a few tablespoons of water to help it wilt.

Makes 3-4 servings.

　1 clove garlic, minced

　½ white onion, diced

　½ pound frozen spinach

　1 tablespoon extra virgin olive oil for cooking

Cook minced garlic and diced onion in olive oil over medium-high heat 4-5 minutes until they become translucent. Be careful not to burn them. Add frozen spinach and cook over medium heat 6-8 minutes until wilted but not browned. Serve warm with breakfast sausage and pesto eggs.

Make It Your Own

- Add a tablespoon of apple cider vinegar, fresh lemon juice, soy sauce or coconut aminos to taste after you have cooked the spinach. If you add them while the spinach is too hot, these sauces can create a sour taste. Add them during the last minute of cooking or after the spinach has been removed from the heat.

- Add organic, nitrate-free bacon crumbles or ham cut in matchsticks to add flavor and protein.

- Try different greens like mustard greens, collard greens or kale.

- Add cubed avocado, diced tomatoes, mushrooms or any other fresh organic vegetable you desire.

# PESTO EGGS

Eggs, they're what's for breakfast. Try adding pesto to your scrambled eggs for a different twist on an old favorite.

2-3 eggs make one serving.

    1 teaspoon extra virgin olive oil for cooking

    2-3 organic eggs

    1 teaspoon *pesto

Heat olive oil over medium-high heat. Scramble eggs and pour into the hot oil, turning gently as the egg starts to cook. Add a teaspoon of pesto or more to taste. Continue to fold the pesto into the egg as it cooks, 1-2 minutes. When the eggs are firm, remove from heat. Serve warm with breakfast sausage and greens.

*Pesto. If you buy premade pesto from the store, look for the one that is greenest in color as it contains more herbs than fat (oils or cheeses). If you make pesto at home, use a blend of garlic, pine nuts, basil and olive oil.

## Make It Your Own

- Concerned about cholesterol? Pesto is great in egg whites alone instead of scrambling the whole egg.

- Eating too much dairy can put you in an unbalanced state. Adding a little parmesan to these eggs if you are not eating too much dairy throughout the week is a tasty way to add flavor and a little protein to this dish.

- This is a great stand alone dish or can be served over leftover fajita steak meat instead of breakfast sausage and greens.

- Try serving this dish with a side of leftover rice and beans.

- Add diced tomatoes or leftover vegetables to the eggs while they are cooking.

# CRUSTLESS GARDEN QUICHE

Quiches are easy to assemble. This one contains protein with the eggs and essential nutrients with the greens.

Makes 4-6 servings.

>    6 organic eggs
>
>    1 tablespoon organic extra virgin olive oil, plus a little more for cooking
>
>    1 clove garlic, minced
>
>    ½ white onion, diced
>
>    ½ pound frozen spinach
>
>    2 tomatoes, one diced, one sliced in rounds

Preheat the oven to 375. In a large mixing bowl, whisk the eggs.

Heat the olive oil over medium-high heat in a frying pan. Add the garlic and onion and cook 4-5 minutes until the onion becomes translucent. Be careful to not burn them. Add the spinach and cook another 5-6 minutes until the spinach has started to wilt. Add one diced tomato to the spinach mixture. Let the spinach mixture cool 3-5 minutes.

Note: if the spinach mixture is still hot when you pour it into the eggs, it can cook the eggs. It's ok if this starts to happen but it is preferable to have the eggs cook in the oven.

Add the slightly cooled spinach mixture to the eggs then pour everything in a lightly oiled square baking dish. Lay thin, round slices of tomato over the top of the quiche. Bake 40-45 minutes or until quiche has cooked through and egg is not runny if a fork or knife is inserted in the quiche.

## Make It Your Own

- Add asparagus, basil or any fresh vegetables or herbs you like to the uncooked mixture before baking.

- Add a dollop of basil pesto to the uncooked mixture before baking.

- Add extra basil leaves on top of the sliced rounds of tomatoes on top of the quiche for a variation on presentation.

- Serve with a side of fresh salsa.

- Serve with a side of fresh fruit.

# CASHEW MILK AND FRESH FRUIT

Native to Brazil, cashew plants take three to five years to develop nuts. They are rich in copper, manganese, magnesium, phosphorous and vitamin K. They contain phytonutrients and antioxidants. One of the healthiest fats you can eat, cashews contain no cholesterol. Unlike most foods that decrease in nutritional value when cooked, the antioxidant activity in cashews actually increases when roasted.

## CASHEW MILK

Soaking the nuts in salt water is a crucial step in this recipe. Soaking the nuts helps break down phytic acid and neutralize enzyme inhibitors, which is important for digestion and nutrient absorption.

   1 cup organic raw cashews

   2-4 cups filtered water

   1 teaspoon sea salt

   1-2 teaspoons raw honey

   1 teaspoon organic cinnamon

Cover the cashews and salt with just enough water to soak. Soak cashews in salt water 2-4 hours. Rinse the soaked cashews thoroughly in running water, taking care to loosen any remaining skins or fibers on the nuts' exteriors.

Put the soaked and rinsed nuts in a blender and blend on low to make a nut butter consistency. This is the base. Add a few teaspoons of water as needed to reach the desired nut butter consistency but do not pour all of the water in at the beginning or you will have a very chunky milk.

Once you have a smooth nut butter consistency, slowly add 1-3 cups of water until you have reached the desired consistency. If you are using the cashew milk as a coffee creamer or wish to freeze it for a non-dairy ice cream, you will want a thicker consistency. If you are using the cashew milk like drinking milk with teas, or to serve with fruit or granola, you will want to add more water to give it a thinner consistency. This recipe is very flexible and forgiving.

Once you have the milk consistency you desire, add the honey and cinnamon. Blend to incorporate ingredients. Chill for a few hours before serving. Serve cold with a side of fresh fruit.

## FRESH FRUIT

Wash and rinse fresh fruit. Serve at room temperature in a bowl.

Make It Your Own

- Make a bowl with granola and bananas and pour the cashew milk over.

- Freeze cashew milk and fresh fruit into popsicles or ice cream.

- Add variations to the cashew milk. Instead of honey and cinnamon, try a small amount of rosewater or lavender water.

# PERFECT CUP OF COFFEE

**M**any of us start our days with our favorite cup of coffee. In recent years, mold has been discovered in a large portion of the coffee supply. As such, it is imperative that you select a brand of coffee that does not have mold. Coffee made from Arabica beans from a high elevation farm are less likely to grow harmful mold.

Prominent biohacker Dave Asprey suggests adding a tablespoon of nutrient-dense, grass-fed unsalted butter, which contains omega-3 fatty acids, more carotenes than a carrot, and vitamins A, D, E and K2. You can also add a dollop of organic coconut oil and honey for additional healthy fats and a sweetened taste. Add cinnamon for a different flavor if you like. This clean cup of coffee with added fats will help distribute the energy slowly and evenly, providing several hours of clean fuel for optimal brain function.

The four main components of the perfect cup of coffee:

1. Clean coffee (no mycotoxins/mold)
2. Grass-fed, unsalted organic butter
3. Organic coconut oil
4. *Honey, vanilla or cinnamon for flavor

*Note: if you are using raw honey for medicinal purposes, the beneficial enzymes are rendered useless when poured in hot coffee. Xylitol is a better choice than agave if you are craving a sweeter cup of joe.

# MID DAY RECIPES

It is important to eat regular, small meals throughout the day to maintain energy levels. If you have a hectic schedule, take time the night before to prepare the next day's lunch so it is ready to grab and go. This helps you avoid unhealthy decisions when you are hungry.

- Important reminders for your midday meals:
- Watch your calories and portion sizes.
- Eat the rainbow.
- Replenish energy reserves with healthy protein.
- Include raw fruits and vegetables.

# ABC Salad: Avocados, Beets and Carrots with Lemon Mustard Sauce

Avocado, Beets and Carrots are the main components of the highly nutritious ABC salad. The avocados provide healthy protein and are high in potassium, folate and vitamins B5, B6, C, E and K. Beets are high in vitamin C, potassium, manganese and folate, while the carrots provide beta carotene, pantothenic acid, folate, potassium, iron, copper, manganese and vitamins A, B8, C, and K. Make the beets the night before to save you time when preparing the salad the next day.

Makes 4-6 servings.

- 2 organic beets, peeled, baked and cubed
- 2 organic avocados, peeled and cubed
- 1 cup organic raw carrots, shredded
- 4 ounces goat cheese, crumbled (optional)
- Mustard dressing, enough to coat
- Mustard dressing
- 2-3 tablespoons dijon mustard
- Juice of one lemon

Wash the beets thoroughly. Wrap them individually in aluminum foil. Bake on 400 for approximately one hour. Allow them to cool and remove the skin.

Cut the beets and avocados into cubes, and place in a large mixing bowl. Add shredded carrots and goat cheese if you are using the cheese.

In a separate bowl, whisk dijon and lemon juice together. Pour mustard dressing over the bowl of vegetables and toss to thoroughly combine. Serve at room temperature or slightly chilled. The salad will keep 2-3 days in the refrigerator. The lemon in the dressing will help prevent the avocado from browning.

# Chicken & Wild Rice Bowl

There are several ways to cook chicken. Frying is on one end of the spectrum, being the least healthiest. Brining might be on the edge as it adds a considerable amount of sodium. The combination of sugars and creatine in the meat, when grilled over high temperatures, creates heterocyclic amines which have the same toxic chemical structure as that found in cigarette smoke. Grilling vegetables does not produce the same toxic effects. Grilling meat occasionally is ok, but you don't want to grill too frequently. The healthiest ways to cook chicken are to bake or boil it. Rotisserie chicken is also a good choice if you do not have time to cook the chicken yourself.

If you're avoiding grains you can replace the rice with a leafy green or spiralized squash and cook appropriately. But if you eat rice, there are several types to consider. We like wild rice for several reasons.

**Health benefits of wild rice:**

- Twice as much protein as brown rice
- Significantly more antioxidants than white rice
- Lower in calories than other rice varieties
- High fiber content assists with healthy digestion
- Good source of phosphorous, zinc and folate
- Good source of vitamins A, C and E
- Gluten and dairy free

## Chicken

Makes 3-4 servings.

   1 organic, skinless, boneless chicken breast

   1-2 teaspoons organic extra virgin olive oil

   1-2 teaspoons *jerk seasonings

*You can purchase jerk seasonings at the grocery store. Read the labels and avoid unnecessary additives. If you would like to make your own jerk seasonings at home, you can try varying amounts of thyme, allspice, turmeric, salt, granulated onion and cayenne.

Preheat oven to 350.

Rinse the chicken breast and pat dry. Rub olive oil over entire chicken breast. Season with jerk seasonings on both sides. Bake for approximately 20 minutes, or until there is no pink

continued

in the middle of the chicken and it has cooked all the way through. If you are not sure how long to cook the chicken, a good rule of thumb when baking chicken is approximately 20 minutes per pound on 350.

Allow chicken to cool to room temperature and slice against the grain into slender strips.

# WILD RICE

Makes 3-4 servings.

  ¼ cup bacon grease

  1 cup organic carrots, shredded

  3 sticks organic celery, chopped in small pieces

  ½ white organic onion, diced fine

  1 ½ cups wild rice

  3-4 cups organic chicken broth

  ¼ cup raw almonds, slivered

  Rinse the rice and set aside.

Cook the carrots, celery and onion in the bacon grease over medium-high heat for 8-10 minutes or until the vegetables have softened. You may use a few tablespoons of olive oil if you prefer instead of the bacon grease.

In a separate pot, bring the chicken broth to boil. Add the rice and lower heat to medium or medium-low to simmer. Cover and simmer approximately 20-30 minutes or until the broth has cooked out and the rice is cooked through.

Pour the cooked rice in a large mixing bowl and add the cooked vegetables and raw almonds. Toss to thoroughly combine.

## Rice Bowl Assembly

Spoon out about a cup of the cooked rice mixture in a serving bowl. Add the sliced cooked chicken on top. Serve warm. This will keep in the refrigerator for 3-4 days, or you can freeze it for several months. You may want to freeze it in individual portions for easy use.

Make It Your Own

- Add bell peppers and jalapeños to give it a more Tex-Mex feel.
- Add black beans for added fiber.
- Serve with white bean and sunbutter hummus (see below).

# WHITE BEAN AND SUNBUTTER HUMMUS

Several hummus recipes call for tahini. We replaced the tahini with nutritious sunbutter. This is a great dip to serve with raw vegetables for dipping: carrots, broccoli, cucumbers, radishes, etc. You can also serve it with the chicken and wild rice bowl above, or as a side to any Mediterranean platter.

Makes 6-8 servings.

2 cans (15-ounces each) organic white cannellini beans

3-4 cloves garlic

1 teaspoon cumin

1 dollop sunbutter

Juice of 1-2 limes

¼–½ cup of organic extra virgin olive oil

Blend everything together in a Vitamix or food processor at high speed. You can adjust the consistency to make it thinner by adding more olive oil as needed. Adjust ingredients according to personal taste. Chill and serve cold.

## Make It Your Own

- Create a Mediterranean platter with the hummus, a variety of olives, charcuterie and cheeses.

- Blend in a roasted beet with the hummus for added nutrition and to make it pink.

- Blend in sriracha, jalapeños, habaneros or other hot peppers to give this a kick.

# GREEN APPLE SLICES TOPPED WITH TUNA SALAD

Albacore tuna is less toxic because it is harvested at a younger age than larger tunas. The younger the fish is harvested, the less time it has spent in potentially toxic waters. We suggest fresh wild-caught Atlantic tuna when possible, as seafood from the Pacific waters are affected with radioactivity from the Fukushima nuclear disaster.

- 1 (5-ounce can) albacore tuna
- 1 tablespoon greek yogurt
- 1 teaspoon apple cider vinegar
- 8-10 organic, seedless, red grapes, halved
- 1-2 tablespoons craisins (dried cranberries)
- 1-2 tablespoons pecans, chopped
- 1 pinch sea salt
- 1 pinch coarse ground black pepper
- Organic green apple, sliced in rounds

Toss all ingredients except the apple together lightly in a mixing bowl to combine. Set aside in the refrigerator to chill 30-40 minutes or up to a few hours.

Slice apples into thin rounds but not too thin; they are the base to hold the tuna salad. Pop any seeds out and discard. Spoon the chilled tuna salad onto each apple round and serve cold.

## Make It Your Own

- Experiment with different varieties of apples: honey crisp, gala, granny smith.
- Experiment with different varieties of grapes: purple, green.
- Replace tuna with chicken for a different protein source.
- Experiment with raisins or dried cherries instead of craisins.

# ADOBO SOUP

This versatile and filling soup offers several options to boost nutrition.

Makes 2-4 servings.

⅓ cup coconut aminos

2-4 garlic cloves, minced

1 tablespoon organic extra virgin olive oil

½ white onion, diced

4-5 cups chicken broth

1 ½–2 ½ cups shredded organic chicken breast

½ pound organic baby bok choy, halved lengthwise and sliced crosswise 1/2-inch wide

½–1 teaspoon cumin, or to taste
½–1 teaspoon chili powder, or to taste
Sea salt, to taste
Coarse ground black pepper, to taste
2 organic green onions, including tender green tops, thinly sliced
Wedges of lime, to taste

Combine the aminos, garlic, olive oil and onion over medium-high heat in a small saucepan. Heat until the onion becomes translucent, about 4-6 minutes. Add chicken broth and bring to a boil. Add chicken and all remaining ingredients except the green onions and lime. Simmer 2-5 minutes until the bok choy is tender. Garnish with green onions and serve with lime wedges.

Make It Your Own

- Substitute spinach or collard greens for the bok choy.
- Replace coconut aminos with low sodium soy sauce.
- Use a yellow or red onion instead of the white onion.
- Add chipotle powder to give it a smokier flavor.

# COLLARD GREEN AND TABBOULEH WRAPS

Anti-inflammatory collard greens are part of the cruciferous vegetable family. They are full of antioxidants and support your body's detoxification process. Firm and hearty yet supple and flexible, they make a great base for a wrap.

Makes 6-8 wraps.

  6-8 large, organic collard green leaves

  1 ½–2 ½ cups cooked quinoa

  1 organic tomato, diced

  ½ organic red onion, diced

  ½ bunch organic fresh parsley, chopped fine

  2-3 tablespoons organic fresh mint, chopped fine

  1 small organic cucumber, diced

  ½–1 cup kalamata olives (seedless)

  ½–1 cup oil-packed sun dried tomatoes, chopped

  Juice of 1-2 organic lemons

  ½ cup organic grapeseed oil

  Sea salt, to taste

  Coarse ground black pepper, to taste

Combine all ingredients besides the collard green leaves in a large bowl and toss to combine thoroughly to make the tabbouleh. Chill tabbouleh until ready to use. When ready to serve, spoon a large amount of tabbouleh into the clean, raw collard green. Wrap it up like a burrito and serve fresh.

## Make It Your Own

- Substitute kale for collard greens.

- Add a deseeded and diced bell pepper for enhanced nutrition and color.

- Add feta cheese for extra protein.

- Substitute avocado oil or olive oil for grapeseed oil.

- Try using your favorite Italian salad dressing instead of the oil and lemon juice.

- Try blanching the collard greens slightly if you do not like the taste of them raw. Do not overcook, or it will become too tender to hold the tabbouleh as a wrap.

# Fig, Chorizo and Goat Cheese Salad

This kale-based salad is rich in flavor and nutrients. Substitute different ingredients to 'make it your own'.

Makes 2-4 servings.

1 small bunch organic kale
1 cup fresh figs, quartered
1 shallot, sliced thin
1 log of hard chorizo (cooked), sliced in bite-sized chunks
Goat cheese in bite-sized chunks, to taste
Juice of 1 lemon
Sea salt, to taste
Coarse ground black pepper, to taste

Crisp kale in a large saucepan over high heat until edges darken. Remove from heat and toss in a salad bowl with all remaining ingredients to combine thoroughly. Serve at room temperature.

Make It Your Own

- Substitute spinach or field greens instead of kale.
- Add a different salad dressing of choice.
- Remember to eat the rainbow: add different vegetables or fruits for different nutritional value. Raw watermelon, radishes, steamed asparagus or grilled peaches all add color and nutrition.

# DINNER RECIPES

Dinner is the last meal of the day and the last opportunity for nutrition to enter your body before you go to sleep. It should also be your lightest meal of the day because we are typically less active at the end of the day. Whatever calories you eat are more likely to be stored instead of burned since you typically go to sleep after dinner. Also, eating too close to bedtime increases blood sugar which can negatively affect sleep patterns. Ideally, you should eat dinner at least three hours before you go to bed. If you have time for a quick after dinner walk, it will help with your digestion before you go to sleep.

# CHICKEN IN ONION MARINADE WITH VEGETABLES

This versatile recipe is a great summer dish that is packed full of nutrients. There are ample ways to make it your own, and several great options to use the leftovers. The onion marinade is the secret weapon of this dish, containing healing turmeric, ginger and other spices. The key thing to remember with the medicinal value of spices is they are only as healthy for you as they are in quality condition. A freshly dried spice that you grind up will have more nutritive properties than a dried spice you have had in your spice cabinet for years.

Grilling is not recommended to do everyday. However, we feel grilling on occasion is not problematic to long-term health. Instead of grilling, you can pan-fry or bake the marinated chicken.

If you need to avoid nightshades, you can easily replace the peppers with any vegetable you prefer.

Makes 4-6 servings.

---

## CHICKEN

2 boneless, skinless chicken breasts

About 2 cups onion marinade

Rinse the chicken and put it in a plastic bag full of the onion marinade to soak for 30 minutes to an hour. You can let the chicken soak in the marinade all day or all night as long as it is refrigerated.

Bake the chicken at 350 degrees for 30-45 minutes, until done and there is no pink in the middle of the chicken.

If you prefer to grill the chicken, grill evenly, about 10 minutes on each side or until the internal temperature has reached 165 F and there is no pink. You can skewer strips of the chicken breast to grill or grill the whole breast intact.

Ideas for Leftovers

1. Make fajitas:
   - Heat up some almond flour tortillas.
   - Fill tortillas with the leftover chicken and veggies.
   - Fold into a taco shape.
   - Top with a sliced avocado or spoonful of guacamole and salsa.
   - Serve warm.

continued

# Onion Marinade

2 white onions, peeled and quartered

8-10 garlic pods, peeled

2 teaspoons turmeric

2 teaspoons ginger

2 teaspoons black pepper

2 teaspoons coriander

½ teaspoon cayenne

1 teaspoon cumin

Blend all ingredients together in a high powered blender or food processor and blend until thoroughly blended. If needed, add a little oil or water to loosen the mixture so it will blend easier, but don't add too much. You want the marinade to be a thick paste consistency. Reserve a few tablespoons of the marinade for the vegetables.

# Vegetables

1 organic zucchini, sliced in rounds

1 organic tomato, sliced in rounds

1 organic red bell pepper, sliced in ½-inch squares

1 organic yellow bell pepper, sliced in ½-inch squares

1-2 tablespoons onion marinade

Salt, to taste

Preheat oven to 375.

Layer the vegetables in a row, alternating colors. Spoon a few tablespoons of the onion marinade over the top of the vegetables. Bake at 375 for about 40 minutes. Add salt to taste and serve warm.

Ideas for Leftovers

2. Make soup:
   - Cube chicken.
   - Reheat veggies and cubed chicken in a tablespoon of olive oil over medium-high heat.
   - Add 4-6 cups of water and 3-4 cubes of chicken bouillon.
   - Bring soup to a boil then reduce heat to simmer on medium 15-20 minutes.
   - Garnish with cilantro, lime wedge and fresh chopped onion.
   - Serve warm.

3. Make nachos:
   - Place leftover chicken slices and veggies on tortilla chips.
   - Add cheese and jalapeños, to taste.
   - Bake uncovered in an oven on 375 until cheese is melted.
   - Serve warm.

4. Make a casserole:
   - Slice remaining chicken.
   - Put chicken slices and remaining veggies in an oiled casserole dish.
   - Add any fresh herbs or seasonings.
   - Bake uncovered in an oven on 375 for 20-30 minutes.

# German Sausage, Potatoes, Asparagus, Sauerkraut and Pickles with Mustard Sauce

Red meat is only recommended to eat once or twice a week to maintain cardiovascular health. Be sure to balance the rest of your meals this week with different lean proteins such as fish, seafood, turkey or chicken. If this is your night for red meat, a great organic, nitrate-free German sausage makes a tasty protein base for the rest of this meal.

Potatoes cooked in chicken stock provide fiber, vitamin B6 and vitamin C, as well as potassium, copper, manganese, phosphorous and niacin. Asparagus contains folate, chromium and vitamins A, C, E and K. The sauerkraut is also a source of vitamins A, C, E, K and B vitamins as well as iron, manganese, copper, magnesium and calcium. Pickles, depending on the brand you select, contain trace minerals and vitamins as well.

Makes 3-4 servings.

---

## Sausage

    1 large link organic, nitrate-free German sausage

    1 teaspoon organic extra virgin olive oil, for cooking

Pan sear the link on medium-high heat in a little bit of olive oil for approximately 5-6 minutes on both sides, until meat has cooked through. Slice in links or rounds and set aside to plate later.

## Potatoes

    12-18 miniature organic potatoes

    4-5 cups chicken broth

Scrub potatoes clean and rinse with running water. Bring 4-5 cups of chicken broth to a boil over high heat. Add the cleaned potatoes to the boiling water and reduce heat slightly to create a slow rolling boil so that the broth does not spill over the sides.

Boil 10-15 minutes, or until potatoes are tender if a fork is inserted in them. Once cooked to desired level of doneness, remove from heat, drain and set aside.

# Asparagus

1 bunch of asparagus

1 cup water

Wash asparagus thoroughly and rinse with running water. Pour water into a pan and turn on medium-high heat. Place the asparagus in the water that is heating up. Some prefer asparagus more crispy, and others more done. Steam asparagus 5-6 minutes, or until you have reached a desired consistency. The longer you cook the asparagus, the creamier it will be. The shorter you cook the asparagus, the crunchier it will be. Once it is done cooking, drain and set aside.

# Sauerkraut and Pickles

There are several great recipes out there for you to explore making sauerkraut and pickles at home. If you are purchasing these items from the grocery store, select organic brands with the lowest amount of sugar and additives. Try to find the most wholesome product on the shelf that has the least number of ingredients.

# Mustard Sauce

2 tablespoons dijon mustard

1 lime

You can double this recipe to make more as needed. Whisk until thoroughly combined and store any remaining sauce in the refrigerator.

## Plate and Serve

Place the sausage, potatoes and asparagus on each plate. Place the sauerkraut and pickle in a separate bowl on each plate. You can either pour the mustard sauce over the asparagus, or you can put it in individual dipping bowls for each guest.

Make It Your Own

- Experiment with different flavors of sausage.
- Replace sausage with a different protein of your choice.
- Remove the sausage for a vegetarian dinner.
- Try using a lemon instead of a lime in the mustard sauce.
- Try using different mustards instead of dijon.
- Use leftover asparagus and sausage in a breakfast quiche.
- Mash or twice-bake leftover potatoes.

# CHICKEN STRIPS WITH HONEY MUSTARD AND PECANS, ROSEMARY SWEET POTATOES & GARLIC, GINGER BROCCOLI

This dinner offers simple, basic ingredients (chicken, sweet potatoes, broccoli) and utilizes pecans, rosemary and garlic to add flavor and anti-inflammatory nutrition.

Lean, organic chicken breasts are low in fat and high in protein, making them a great choice for anyone working on maintaining healthy weight. Sweet potatoes are a low cost option that pack a lot of nutrition into one serving. They are an easy way to incorporate 'orange' if you are eating the rainbow, and they contain a plethora of vitamins and minerals including B6, C and D. Organic broccoli is also rich in vitamins and nutrients such as C, beta carotene, K, Bs, folate, potassium and fiber. Did you know that one cup of broccoli contains approximately the same amount of vitamin C as one orange?

Pecans are loaded with vitamins and minerals. Adding them to chicken strips gives added crunch and nutrition. Pecans are a healthy fat, high in fiber and contain protein, manganese, phosphorous, magnesium, iron and several other nutrients. They are anti-inflammatory and a great nut to have on hand to incorporate into your recipes.

Rosemary is a great anti-inflammatory herb to have in your pantry or in your garden. Rosemary stimulates circulation, improves digestion and stimulates the immune system. It is hearty and easy to grow, not requiring much attention.

Garlic is the go-to plant for antibacterial, antioxidant and anti-inflammatory medicinal purposes. It tastes great and contains vitamins B6 and C as well as selenium and manganese.

Makes 3-4 servings.

---

## CHICKEN STRIPS

- 2-3 tablespoons dijon
- 2-3 tablespoons raw, organic honey
- 1 organic chicken breast
- 1-2 cups pecans, chopped

Preheat the oven to 375. Whisk the dijon and honey together and separate into two small bowls and set aside. Rinse the chicken breast and cut into strips. Pat dry and set aside. Chop pecans into small pieces and set aside in a small bowl.

### Make It Your Own

- Try boiling and mashing the sweet potatoes for a different way to make them. Try adding boiled and mashed carrots to blend in some extra "orange" nutrition.

- Replace the coconut amino acids with a soy sauce or other asian flavored sauce, being careful to read the ingredient label and make healthy choices.

continued

Dip the chicken breast in one of the honey mustard sauces and roll in the pecans. Lay strips on a greased baking sheet. Sprinkle any extra pecan pieces on top of the strips to coat completely. Bake for about 20 minutes or until there is no pink and the pecans have started to crisp. Serve warm with a side dipping bowl of the remaining honey mustard sauce that was not used to dress the chicken.

## ROSEMARY SWEET POTATOES

    2-3 large sweet potatoes

    Extra virgin olive oil cooking spray

    3-4 sprigs fresh rosemary (or 1 tablespoon dried)

    1-2 teaspoons ground cinnamon

    2-3 tablespoons raw pumpkin seeds

Preheat oven to 400. Wash sweet potatoes and slice into thin rounds. Layer rounds in a log shape in a baking dish.

Spray the sweet potatoes with olive oil cooking spray to lightly coat and sprinkle all remaining ingredients on top to give the dish a rustic look. Bake 40-50 minutes or until sweet potatoes are tender. Serve warm with honey mustard pecan chicken and garlic, ginger broccoli.

## GARLIC, GINGER BROCCOLI

    1 head organic broccoli, chopped

    1 2-inch piece organic ginger, minced

    2-3 cloves garlic, minced

    1-2 tablespoons coconut amino acids

Preheat the oven to 400. Wash and rinse the broccoli. Chop it into small bite-sized pieces and place in a bowl. Add minced garlic and ginger. Add coconut aminos and toss all ingredients, to thoroughly coat. Pour broccoli mixture into a greased or nonstick baking dish and bake for approximately 20-25 minutes, or until broccoli has reached desired crispy consistency. Serve with rosemary sweet potatoes and honey mustard pecan chicken.

Ideas for Leftovers

- Keep some extra pecans around to add to salads, granolas or snacks.

- Turn leftover broccoli into a quiche.

- Store leftover fresh rosemary by freezing it in olive oil in ice cube trays to be able to pop out and use in cooking as needed.

- Freeze leftover rosemary with lemonade in an ice cube tray to make herbal lemon ice cubes to use in teas or juice blends.

# Atlantic Salmon and Mango Avocado Salsa

Since radiation from the Fukushima nuclear disaster has crossed the Pacific all the way to waters off the United States' coast, we now find some Pacific seafood contains harmful radioactive cancer-causing Cesium-137 and Strontium-90. For that reason, we currently recommend eating only Atlantic Salmon at the time of the writing of this book.

This salmon and salsa recipe has an island-themed flavor. You can make fish tacos with a great almond flour tortilla or serve with a green vegetable of choice such as steamed asparagus or garlic, ginger broccoli as seen earlier.

Makes 4 servings.

## Salmon

4 filets Atlantic salmon

3-4 tablespoons organic teriyaki sauce

Bring the salmon to room temperature and dip both sides in your choice of teriyaki sauce. Place each filet skin side up in a nonstick skillet. Pan fry over medium-high heat on one side, approximately 4-5 minutes. Use a spatula to turn each filet over to cook on the other side another 4-5 minutes, pouring extra teriyaki sauce as desired for additional flavor. Serve warm, with the skin on, skin side down with a side of mango avocado salsa.

## Mango Avocado Salsa

2 organic mangos, diced

2 organic avocados, diced

1-2 organic tomatoes, diced

½–1 organic jalapeño, deseeded, deveined and diced

1 bunch cilantro, de-stemmed and chopped

Juice of 1-2 limes

Sea salt, to taste

Cracked black pepper, to taste

Place all ingredients in a serving bowl and toss lightly to combine. Taste and modify ingredients according to taste before serving.

### Make It Your Own

- Try different varieties of heirloom tomatoes to give the salsa a nice variation in color.

- Make fish tacos with the fish and salsa and a wedge of lime.

- Cook the fish according to your preference: pan fry, grill or bake it.

# BONE BROTH

Bone broth has been popularized in recent years due to its amino acids, collagen, gelatin and trace minerals. Since you are trying to get the most nutritional value from this soup, it is important to use proper cooking equipment. Large stainless steel soup pots or older crock pots that contain toxic alloys will taint your healthy soup. Instead, use a ceramic crock pot and cook over low temperature for a long time. Do not skip the vinegar, as this is what pulls the minerals out of the bones and into the soup. Dog owners please note: raw bones are safe to give most dogs, but cooked bones will splinter and cause major problems.

Makes 6-8 servings.

Recipe uses an 8 ½ quart ceramic crock pot.

1-2 tablespoons organic extra virgin olive oil

3 pounds (variety of meaty and non-meaty) grass-fed beef bones: knuckle, rib, tail or neck bones

¼ cup vinegar

Water, enough to fill half the crock pot

2-3 organic carrots, chopped rough

2-3 cloves garlic, minced

1 white onion, chopped rough

2-3 sticks organic celery, chopped rough

Sea salt, to taste

Pour organic extra virgin olive oil into a large skillet over medium-high to high heat. Brown meaty bones thoroughly on all sides in the oil. Put browned bones in the crock pot with vinegar, vegetables and enough water to cover about half of the pot, leaving room for the soup to grow. Pour a little water into the pan where the bones were browning and heat slightly to deglaze the pan, or loosen the browned bits and add them to the crock pot.

Make sure the lid is sealed properly to contain heat. Turn the heat on high until the broth starts to get bubbly then reduce to low. Cook at least eight hours but you may wish to continue cooking for 12 hours or longer. Taste and make seasoning adjustments as desired. Skim fat globules out of the soup and serve warm.

Make It Your Own
- Use different types of bones.
- Roast bones in the oven instead of pan frying before you put them in the crock pot.
- Simmer longer to change the flavor.

# Lemon Garlic Shrimp

Shrimp is a great source of protein that contains omega-3 fatty acids, with balanced amounts of DHA and EPA, two important omega-3s. They also contain energizing vitamin B12 in addition to several other vitamins. They are easy to cook and can be made several different ways.

Makes 3-4 servings.

1 ½–2 pounds shrimp, peeled and deveined

2-3 tablespoons organic extra virgin olive oil

4-5 tablespoons grass-fed organic butter, melted

3-4 garlic cloves, minced

Juice of 2-3 organic lemons

1 teaspoon coconut aminos

1 teaspoon lemon pepper seasoning

3-4 tablespoons chopped fresh parsley

Preheat oven to 400.

Rub shrimp in olive oil then place in a shallow baking dish. Pour all remaining ingredients in a bowl except the parsley and stir to combine. Pour mixture over the shrimp and bake 8-10 minutes or until the shrimp have cooked through.

Serve with a sliced avocado over field greens or in your favorite pasta.

Make It Your Own

- Try adding different flavors to your shrimp instead of garlic and lemon such as:
- Tomato and basil
- Barbecue sauce and bacon
- Orange, honey and jalapeño

# CURRIED CASHEW CAULIFLOWER WITH TOMATOES ROCKEFELLER

Hearty vegetables are a meal in and of themselves. Cauliflower is great raw or cooked. One serving contains almost 80% of the daily recommended amount of vitamin C. It helps with brain health, heart health, digestion and detoxification all while reducing inflammation.

Makes 4 servings.

# CURRIED CASHEW CAULIFLOWER

1 head organic cauliflower, broken into bite-sized pieces

1 cup raw cashews

1-2 tablespoons macadamia nut oil

1-2 teaspoons paprika

1-2 teaspoons cayenne

1-2 cups creamy curry sauce

Preheat oven to 400. Rub the cauliflower bits and cashews in cooking oil to coat thoroughly. Sprinkle paprika and cayenne over oiled cauliflower and cashews on a cookie sheet. Bake 20-30 minutes or until the ends become roasted and cauliflower is at the desired texture. Baking longer will soften the cauliflower more. Remove from the oven and allow to cool slightly. Toss the roasted cauliflower and cashews in a bowl with your favorite brand of curry sauce. Serve warm.

# TOMATOES ROCKEFELLER

4 organic Roma tomatoes

1 (10-ounce) package organic frozen spinach with onions

2 organic free-range eggs

1-2 cloves garlic, minced

1 cup gluten-free bread crumbs

1-2 teaspoons Worcestershire sauce

1-2 teaspoons Italian seasoning

Preheat oven to 400.

Wash and hollow out 4 roma tomatoes. Chop the bottoms flat so they can stand alone as a bowl. Set aside the tomato insides.

Wilt spinach over medium-high heat for 6-8 minutes or until cooked but not mushy. In a separate large mixing bowl, scramble the eggs. Add the spinach to the eggs along with the garlic, bread crumbs, Worcestershire sauce, tomato insides and Italian seasoning. Mix to combine thoroughly and set aside.

Stand tomato bowls up on an oiled baking sheet. Fill tomato bowls with spinach mixture and bake 10-15 minutes, or until edges start to crisp and the egg has cooked through.

Make It Your Own

- Use organic extra virgin olive oil, or your preferred cooking oil to coat the cauliflower and cashews.

- Add chunks of butternut squash to the cauliflower dish for added nutrients.

- Try peanuts instead of cashews to the cauliflower.

- Instead of stuffing the tomatoes, try putting the spinach mixture on top of slices of tomatoes.

- Top tomatoes rockefeller with shaved parmesan cheese.

- If you can't find frozen spinach that contains onions, just add about ½ a raw onion, diced finely to the spinach when you are cooking it.

- Replace worcestershire sauce with coconut aminos.

# PRE WORKOUT RECIPES

Fueling up with healthy energy like natural sugars, electrolytes and proteins will give your body enough energy to complete a great workout. Be sure to drink plenty of water to stay hydrated before, during and after any workout.

## Ideas to Supercharge Your Workout

- Oatmeal with apples and cinnamon
- Granola in almond milk with fresh fruit
- Peanut butter on apple slices
- Boiled egg
- Trail mix
- Granola bar

# BANANA BAR

Bananas are a great midday snack because they are naturally packed with nutrition, fiber and natural sugars to boost your energy for the rest of the afternoon. Bananas contain potassium, pectin (a form of fiber), magnesium and vitamins C and B6. They also contain helpful antioxidants which helps your body neutralize excessive free radicals.

In this banana bar, you can choose your preferred butter and toppings. Each of the different toppings and butters provide an added dose of nutrition to this snack. If you have leftovers, just pop them into the blender and make a smoothie. You can drink the smoothie right away, or freeze it to use later.

Serving size: 1 banana makes 1 serving.

  1 banana, sliced into rounds

## Instructions

Spread a dollop of your preferred butter on each banana round and sprinkle any topping you like on top of the butter. Serve with a side of fresh fruit such as orange slices or apple slices.

Choose your own butter
  Sunbutter
  Peanut butter
  Almond butter
  Nutella

Choose your own toppings
  Coconut cashew (or any flavor) granola
  Walnut halves
  Macadamia nuts
  Pecan halves
  Almonds
  Dried fruit: cherries, strawberries, apricots
  Dark chocolate
  Cacao
  Pumpkin seeds
  Sunflower seeds

# BANANA ALMOND SMOOTHIE

Bananas offer much needed potassium while walnuts and almond butter provide protein. Both will assist with muscle health while you are working out. Modify this recipe as desired to use other healthy ingredients.

Makes 1-2 servings.

  1 frozen organic banana

  1-2 cups almond milk

  1 tablespoon raw, organic honey

  ¼ cup almond butter

  1 teaspoon vanilla

  Blend everything on high until smooth.

Make It Your Own

- Substitute sunbutter or peanut butter for almond butter.

- Substitute another non-dairy milk for the almond milk.

# KIWI, CASHEW, KALE SMOOTHIE

Superfruit kiwi contains several nutrients, including five times as much vitamin C as an orange. Add in protein-filled cashews and nutritious kale and this smoothie will fuel you up for a great workout.

  1-2 cups cashew milk

  1-2 cups organic kale

  1-2 kiwi fruits, peeled

  1 tablespoon sunbutter

  1 teaspoon raw organic honey

Make It Your Own

- Substitute maple syrup or agave for the honey.

- Alternate your favorite nut butters and milks according to what you have on hand in your pantry.

- Make your own cashew milk

# WATERMELON AND GOLDEN BEET SALAD

Sea salted watermelon is a tasty way to replenish your body's electrolyte reserves. Golden beets are rich in fiber, iron and potassium as well as beta carotene and vitamins A and C. Pistachios add healthy fat, protein and minerals as well.

Makes 3- 4 servings.

- ½ watermelon, deseeded and cubed
- 2-3 golden beets
- 1 cup pistachios
- 1 teaspoon grapeseed oil
- Juice of ½ organic lemon
- Sea salt, to taste

Preheat oven to 400. Bake beets for 40-50 minutes or until cooked through. Cool slightly and remove skin while the beets are still warm. Set aside and allow to cool 20-30 minutes. Once cooled, cut the beets into cubes.

Toss watermelon, beets, pistachios, oil, lemon and sea salt in a large mixing bowl. Chill and serve cold.

## Make It Your Own

- Add colorful and healthy watermelon, radishes or figs to boost nutrition and flavor.
- Add bacon or another protein for more fuel.
- Add goat cheese or your favorite cheese for added fats.
- Add field greens or spinach.

# POST WORKOUT RECIPES

A good workout can leave you dehydrated and depleted. Make sure you drink plenty of filtered water before, during and after your workout. You will want to replenish nutrients, electrolytes and proteins that were burned up during your workout so your body can repair muscle tissue and refuel for the rest of the day.

---

## BUTTERNUT SQUASH WITH PESTO AND BACON

High in potassium and vitamin B6, butternut squash makes a great after-workout meal. Add protein with bacon and walnuts along with flavor and medicinal qualities with the basil pesto. Make the pesto with your favorite recipe at home or purchase it from the grocery store premade. If buying from the store, look for the brand with the least amount of additives and the freshest green color.

Makes 2 servings.

    1 organic butternut squash, deseeded and halved

    2 tablespoons organic butter

    2 tablespoons basil/garlic pesto

    3-4 pieces organic, nitrate-free bacon, cooked and crumbled

    Small handful of walnuts

Preheat oven to 400. Wash and rinse butternut squash halves, placing them open side up on a baking dish. Put a tablespoon of butter in each half and bake 30-40 minutes or until squash is tender and done. Remove and allow squash to cool.

Cube cooled squash and put in a mixing bowl with the remaining ingredients, adjusting levels to accommodate personal taste. Toss everything lightly, being careful not to mash the squash and maintain the integrity of the cubes. Eat warm, or refrigerate.

### Make It Your Own

- Explore using different herbs if you do not have any pesto.

- Use different nuts.

- Refrigerate in individual serving sizes and take it along to your workout so it's ready to eat immediately.

# Spiralized Zucchini Caprese with Sliced Turkey

Spiralizers are readily available at many grocery stores and online. In the absence of a spiralizer at home, you can purchase spiralized vegetables at the grocery store. You can also buy small balls of mozzarella in Italian herbs and seasonings that work well with this dish.

Makes 1-2 servings.

- 3-4 slices organic deli turkey breast
- 1 teaspoon organic extra virgin olive oil
- 1 organic zucchini, spiralized (or 1 small container)
- 6-10 organic cherry tomatoes, halved
- 4-6 chunks of fresh mozzarella
- 1-2 tablespoons Italian dressing

Slice the turkey in matchstick sizes and sear in olive oil over medium-high heat for a few minutes until the edges start to crisp. Remove from heat and set aside.

Once the turkey has cooled, toss it with remaining ingredients in a serving bowl to coat everything thoroughly. Adjust seasonings to taste. Serve room temperature or chilled.

Make It Your Own

- Substitute your favorite protein instead of the turkey.
- Use leftovers to make an omelette, quiche or breakfast casserole.
- Use Italian spices and organic extra virgin olive oil instead of Italian dressing.

# BACON WRAPPED STUFFED DATES

Dates contain essential minerals and vitamins. They are a great source of natural sugar, energy and fiber. Add a little protein to these healthy fruits and you have a great post-workout snack that replenishes energy. These also make great additions to any potluck meal. You will need toothpicks to help make this recipe.

Makes 4-6 servings.

    1 package dates, pitted

    A few dollops of sunbutter

    ½ package bacon

    Sea salt, to taste

Preheat oven to 375.

Stuff dates with sunbutter like a miniature loaded potato. Add sea salt if your sunbutter is bland. Wrap half a slice of raw bacon around the stuffed date, using toothpicks to hold the bacon in place. Bake 15-20 minutes then rotate so the bacon cooks thoroughly. Bake an additional 15-20 minutes until bacon has crisped around the edges. Serve warm, or store refrigerated and eat as desired for a tasty snack.

Make It Your Own

- Add a dried cranberry or raisin on top of the sunbutter for added flare and a little extra nutrition.

- Substitute any of your favorite nut butters in place of the sunbutter.

For an extra savory treat, try adding blue cheese or chorizo instead of nut butters.

# DESSERTS

Some people are more inclined to have a 'sweet tooth,' or a desire for sweet-flavored foods due to genetic preferences and hormonal cravings. Some choices such as cacao are nutritionally beneficial while providing an emotional payoff by boosting positive feelings.

When deciding to eat sweets, as with anything else, we encourage you to use balance and common sense. Inflammatory desserts that contain white sugar and high fructose corn syrup should be avoided. Instead, we encourage you to explore some new ways to add nutrition to your desserts with some of the recipes we provide in this section.

## BANANA NICE CREAM WITH WALNUTS AND CHOCOLATE CHIPS

This recipe is a great way to utilize ripe bananas. Just mash them up, freeze them and add your favorite toppings for a gluten-free, dairy-free dessert.

Makes 2-3 servings.

   2-3 ripe organic bananas, mashed

   2-3 tablespoons creamy, organic almond butter

   1 teaspoon organic coconut oil

   1 cup almond milk

   ½ teaspoon organic vanilla

   ½ teaspoon ground cinnamon

Blend everything in a food processor and freeze. Serve frozen and top with walnuts and unsweetened dark chocolate chips.

Make It Your Own

- Exchange almond butter for any nut butter of your liking.

- Exchange almond milk for another non-dairy milk of your choice.

- Experiment by adding other ingredients: avocado, cacao, strawberries, blueberries, etc.

# Avocado Chocolate Pudding

Nutrient-dense, anti-inflammatory avocados are a great food to incorporate to make dessert a little healthier.

2 organic avocados, peeled and pitted, shells reserved

½ cup unsweetened cocoa powder

¼ cup raw, organic honey

1 teaspoon organic vanilla

1-2 teaspoons unsweetened chocolate chips, to garnish

Blend everything besides the chocolate chips in a food processor until it reaches a smooth consistency. Chill for 30-40 minutes or overnight and serve cold in avocado shells as the bowl. Garnish with unsweetened chocolate chips.

## Make It Your Own

- Experiment with adding coconut oil or coconut milk to give the pudding a different consistency and more tropical flavor.

- Garnish with shredded coconut flakes as an alternative option.

- Freeze leftovers to make ice cream.

- Add a pinch of sea salt for a salty/sweet flavor combination.

- Experiment with different types of cocoa powder.

# Avocado, Coconut, Mint, Lime and Honey Sherbet

This sweet dessert is light, easy to make and loaded with ingredients that are good for you.

The difference between a sherbet and a sorbet is the sorbets are typically non-dairy. Sherberts are creamier because they contain milk, cream, or something similar to give them a thicker consistency. In this recipe we utilize coconut milk to offer that creamier texture. Coconut milk is lactose-free and a good source of fiber, vitamins C, E, B1, B3, B5 and B6 and minerals including iron, selenium, sodium, calcium, magnesium and phosphorous.

Coconut meat is a nutrient-rich healthy fat that fuels several mechanical functions in your body. If you have not cooked with coconut meat before, it can be sweet and tender or it can be a little bit crunchier. It can be eaten raw, blended into smoothies, cooked or made into preserves.

Makes 3-4 servings.

  2-3 avocados

  Meat from ½ of one coconut

  ½ cup coconut milk

  ¼ cup organic, raw honey

  Juice of 1 small organic lime

  1 small sprig fresh mint, chopped

  1 cup macadamia nuts, chopped

Blend all ingredients besides the macadamia nuts in a food processor. Pour into a container and freeze in the freezer. Once frozen, remove and serve cold. Top with chopped macadamia nuts and a fresh mint leaf.

Make It Your Own
- Add a teaspoon of organic vanilla.
- Add a ripe banana for added nutrients.
- Trade out coconut milk for your favorite nut milk.
- Adjust flavors as you like.

# CHOCOLATE COVERED FRUIT KABOBS

This is an easy dessert to make for kids of all ages to bring to potlucks or picnics. You can turn it into a family activity and get everyone involved. If the chocolate sauce seems too thin, refrigerate after dipping to help it harden on the fruit and repeat dipping / refrigerating rotations until you get the desired coating thickness.

Makes 6 skewers.

## FRUIT

6 slender skewers

1-2 organic bananas

12-18 organic strawberries

12-18 organic blueberries

## CHOCOLATE SAUCE

½ cup cocoa powder

1 cup organic extra virgin coconut oil

⅓ cup raw organic honey

1 teaspoon vanilla

½ teaspoon cinnamon

## TOPPINGS

Coconut flakes, for optional topping

Your choice of crushed nuts, for optional topping

Line a cookie sheet with parchment paper and set aside.

Wash strawberries and blueberries thoroughly and set aside to dry. Peel banana and slice in thick rounds. Skewer fruit in any pattern you like, making a full skewer of bananas, strawberries and blueberries.

Melt chocolate sauce ingredients together on low heat in a shallow skillet.

Dip the skewered fruit into the chocolate sauce. You may wish to add 2-3 layers of the sauce. You can refrigerate between dipping in the chocolate sauce again to help everything harden appropriately. Before the last layer hardens, sprinkle coconut flakes and crushed nuts as desired on top of each fruit piece.

### Make It Your Own

- Experiment with different fruits for the skewer: blackberries, raspberries, grapes, oranges, pineapple, kiwi, etc.

- Add edible herbs to the skewer to add a unique flavor combination such as mint or basil.

- Use different nuts for the topping: peanuts, walnuts, Brazil nuts, macadamia nuts, pistachios, pecans, etc.

# Appendix A
# References and Resources

## Food Allergy and Chemical Sensitivity Testing Centers

You will need a physician's prescription for these tests. These cutting-edge scientific tests will help you identify longstanding unrecognized stressors that when addressed will help you take control of your life.

Your doctor may not even know these companies exist or that these specific tests are available, so you may have to share this information and demand they run the tests for you to either identify or rule out specific issues. Consider these tests an important part of your quest for optimal health. Please take the time to review these specialty testing websites to get a feel for the specific tests you would like to have performed.

### Cell Science Systems

Their goal is to be at the forefront of developing relevant assays/testing for the personalized prevention and care of chronic symptomology and disease through research and development.

> www.ALCAT.com

### Genova Diagnostics

They are a clinical laboratory pioneering a systems approach that supports healthcare providers in the personalized treatment and prevention of chronic disease. Chronic diseases are often complex and Genova's system-based testing helps physicians develop targeted treatments for their patients. Easy-to-read color graphic reports synthesize test results into actionable information and facilitate physician-patient communication.

> www.metametrix.com

## Direct Access Laboratory Testing

In our brave new world, both technology and legislation have advanced to the point where you can take control of your own health and wellness. These websites allow you to go to a local blood draw facility (like Quest or LABCORP) and have your blood drawn. The facility will ship your sample to the lab and in a few days you will get your results via email.

Please note: Direct access lab testing services are not available in MD, NJ, NY or RI.

### Preferred Direct Lab Testing Centers

www.lef.org

www.directlabs.com

www.wellnessfx.com

### Additional Direct Lab Testing Centers

www.healthonelabs.com

www.health-tests-direct.com

www.healthcheckusa.com

### Omega-3 Testing

Test your omega-3 level with one drop of blood.

www.omegaquant.com

### Hair Analysis

While hair analysis should not be used to predict any medical outcomes, the analysis can be beneficial in identifying imbalances in our bodies and exposure to toxins like methylmercury, especially important for expecting mothers. You will need to work with a physician in order to have the hair analysis done.

www.hairanalysisprogram.com

www.traceelements.com/LabServices/SampleCollection.aspx

## Non-Governmental Organizations

These are private organizations we trust that are dedicated to educating and protecting consumers.

### The Weston A. Price Foundation

The Weston A. Price Foundation is dedicated to restoring nutrient-dense foods to the human diet through education, research and activism. It supports a number of movements that contribute to this objective including accurate nutrition instruction, organic and biodynamic farming, pasture-feeding of livestock, community-supported farms, honest and informative labeling, prepared parenting and nurturing therapies.

www.westonaprice.org

## NSF International

NSF International develops public health standards and certification programs that help protect the world's food, water, consumer products and environment.

www.nsf.org

## Consumer Labs

ConsumerLab.com, LLC ("CL") is the leading provider of independent test results and information to help consumers and healthcare professionals identify the best quality health and nutrition products. It publishes results of its tests in comprehensive reports at its website.

www.consumerlab.com

## US Pharmacopeia

The U.S. Pharmacopeial Convention (USP) is a scientific nonprofit organization that sets standards for the identity, strength, quality and purity of medicines, food ingredients and dietary supplements manufactured, distributed and consumed worldwide. USP's drug standards are enforceable in the United States by the Food and Drug Administration, and these standards are used in more than 140 countries.

www.usp.org

## University of Maryland Medical Center

The University of Maryland Medical Center provides an up to date guide of complementary and alternative medical protocols through its online Complementary and Alternative Medicine Guide.

umm.edu/health/medical/altmed

# Household & Cosmetic Toxicology Resources

These references and ideas will help you keep your household environment clean as well as avoid harmful chemical toxins in cleaners and cosmetics.

1. Check your home environment using testing kits you can purchase at your local hardware store. PRO-LAB® is one popular brand. Tests include: mold, radon gas, water, allergens, carbon monoxide, lead paint and pesticides

   a. Additional Water testing site: www.ntllabs.com

2. Contact local companies who can run tests for allergens, molds, chemicals and toxins within your home.

3. We support the "WholeFoods Quality Standards." You don't have to shop at WholeFoods® to adhere to these standards, but they are as good a reference as you can get for food, soaps and cosmetics. www.wholefoodsmarket.com/quality-standards

4. We support cross-checking government standards with those of reputable non-government organizations like those listed above. This cosmetics database from the Environmental Working Group is a great way to review individual ingredients in soaps and cosmetics for what they call hazards, which are ranked from 1 (low hazard) to 10 (high hazard). www.ewg.org/skindeep

## Governmental Organizations

Review the government websites below from agencies responsible for our food safety or which offer details on food and food products. You can use these websites for further research as well as food safety notifications.

USDA–Natural Agricultural Library fnic.nal.usda.gov

U.S. National Library of Medicine www.nlm.nih.gov

U.S. Food and Drug Administration www.fda.gov

Centers for Disease Control and Prevention www.cdc.gov

PubMed www.ncbi.nlm.nih.gov/pubmed

National Center for Complementary and Integrative Health nccih.nih.gov

## Our Favorite Websites

- Biohacking: Dave Asprey: www.bulletproofexec.com
- Rewilding Pioneer: Daniel Vitalis: www.danielvitalis.com
- Author Jesse Cannone: www.losethebackpain.com
- Author Tiffany Harelik: www.tiffanyharelik.com

# Appendix B
# Our Favorite Books
# Supporting the 4 Pillars of
# The Complete Healing Formula™

## Physical
- *The 7-Day Back Pain Cure* by Jesse Cannone
- *Why We Hurt* by Dr Greg Fors
- *How to Eat, Move and Be Healthy!* by Paul Chek

## Emotional
- *The Biology of Belief* by Bruce Lipton
- *Virus of the Mind* by Richard Brodie
- *The Hidden Messages in Water* by Masaru Emoto
- *Molecules of Emotion* by Candace Pert

## Nutritional
- *Nourishing Broth: An Old-Fashioned Remedy for the Modern World* by Sally Fallon Morell and Kaayla T. Daniel
- *Nourishing Traditions: The Cookbook that Challenges Politically Correct Nutrition and the Diet Dictocrats* by Sally Fallon and Mary Enig
- *The Blood Sugar Solution*, Mark Hyman, MD
- *Win the War Within* by Floyd H. Chilton, Ph.D.
- *Everything You Need to Know About Enzymes* by Tom Bohager
- *Micro Miracles: Discover the Healing Power of Enzymes* by Ellen W. Cutler, DC

- *The Calcium Lie* by Dr. Robert Thompson and Kathleen Barnes
- *The China Study* by Dr. T. Colin Campbell
- *The Whole Soy Story* by Kaayla T. Daniel
- *The Cure for All Diseases* by Dr. Hulda Clark
- *Food Politics: How the Food Industry Influences Nutrition and Health* by Marion Nestle
- *In Defense of Food: An Eater's Manifesto* by Michael Pollan
- *Ratio: The Simple Codes Behind the Craft of Everyday Cooking* by Michael Ruhlman

## Spiritual

- *Zero Limits: The Secret Hawaiian System for Wealth, Health, Peace, and More* by Joe Vitale
- *Infinite Self* by Stuart Wilde
- *The Alchemist* by Paulo Coelho
- *The Power of Now* by Eckhart Tolle
- *The Art of Happiness* by Dalai Lama and Howard Cutler

# Appendix C
# 7 Common Nutritional Imbalances

In its simplest form, The Complete Healing Formula™ helps you identify and correct imbalances in your body to allow you to heal. In this book we focus primarily on the area of nutrition.

If you have read this far you now understand the basic concepts regarding food, supplements and requirements for restoring nutritional balance. We support education over external control, so... good news! You no longer have to rely on someone else to tell you what you can and can not eat, regardless of your current condition.

The purpose of this appendix is to get you to think, to get you to look at how you eat, and to understand that everything matters, even the little things by sharing seven common imbalances few consider on their own. Use them as a guidepost to look at your diet and ask yourself, "Do I have an imbalance in this area? Where else can I find hidden imbalances in my diet?"

Our hope is that by taking corrective actions to restore balance in your diet you will quickly experience healing, pain relief and return to living an optimal life...

## 1. Protein Intake vs Types of Fatty Acids

The proteins you eat may be the key to your recovery. There are several considerations when choosing proteins, such as animal vs plant proteins and lean vs fatty meats. Even the method chosen to cook the protein matters. However, different protein sources have different blends of another key nutritional component: fatty acids.

Pork, beef, poultry as well as nuts and seeds are all great sources of protein. They're also typically higher in omega-6 fatty acids than omega-3 fatty acids. Both are essential, but some experts believe we should keep close to a 1:1 ratio. Higher than a 4:1 ratio of omega-6 to omega-3 fatty acids leads to health problems. Yet the average American diet contains 14 to 25 times more omega-6 fatty acids than omega-3 fatty acids.

This highly prevalent imbalance between omega-6 and omega-3 fatty acids means you should actively seek out protein sources high in omega-3s and monitor your omega-6 intake. Make that doubly important when you are inflamed and in pain as balancing that ratio may have an enormous impact on your health.

Please consider adding your favorite fish for a blast of omega-3 several times per week. Mackerel, salmon and cod top the list. Omega-3 fortified eggs are another option. If you like red meat, choose grass-fed beef which has about a 3:1 ratio of omega-6 to omega-3 (compared to 20:1 or higher ratio for grain-fed). Good plant sources of omega-3s include flaxseed, walnuts, chia seeds and hemp. These are high in the alpha-linoleic acid (ALA) form of omega-3.

Remember, food first, supplement second. But if you are one of those who eat 25 times as much omega-6, you need to have a good long talk with your doctor about supplementing with omega-3. It may just be the single most important nutritional change you can make.

It's a good idea to test your omega-3 levels on a regular basis. You can do so with one drop of blood through the testing service available at www.omegaquant.com

## 2. Sea Salt vs Table Salt and Iodine

We prefer any of the various types of sea salt over table salt, but like anything else, there runs a risk of an imbalance. Table salt has become the primary source of iodine in today's diet so if you switch from table salt high in iodine to only sea salt low in iodine, you will need to find another source for your iodine.

Cod fish, yogurt, milk, shrimp and eggs are all decent sources of iodine. If you're concerned about iodine deficiency, seaweed like kelp, nori, kombu and wakame has some of the most abundant iodine available in food form.

## 3. Water Intake vs Lifestyle

Everything matters when it comes to healing. This includes your water intake. Your lifestyle will affect your body's water requirements. The list below are only some of the considerations you should take into account when planning or how much water you should drink on a daily basis.

- Seasonal consideration
- Inside (A/C or Heat)
- Outside (hot and humid or cold and windy)
- Environment (work, home and travel)
- Health consideration

- Medications or supplements
- Pregnancy or breastfeeding
- Intensity of exercise
- What else you are eating or drinking that day

Of course this list is incomplete as there are many factors unique to your life, but the point is to get you to think. Consider these scenarios to decide if you may need to change your drinking habits:

- If you work outside, whether in heat or cold, and you do not pee for hours, you are not drinking enough.

- If your urine is less than clear, you are not drinking enough, (except first thing in the morning or after taking some medications and supplements)

- If you are taking medications or supplements and you are constipated, you are not drinking enough.

- If you drink alcohol, you run a risk of becoming dehydrated.

- If you drink coffee or other caffeinated drinks, you run a risk of becoming dehydrated.

- If you eat high levels of protein, you need to make sure your kidneys can process that much protein. Consider having your doctor conduct a urinalysis, but as a rule drink more water when you eat more protein.

Like anything else there is no single amount or specific gauge for any one person, so train yourself to be aware of the signs and keep drinking enough water every day. You just may find your body in a better state, very soon.

## 4. Vitamins and Minerals

There probably isn't a single person in the industrious world who does not believe vitamins and minerals are important for your health. But to reinforce the message of this book, your body will never fully heal itself when your body has a nutritional imbalance. Knowing the difference between not enough, just enough and more than enough in regards to your vitamin and mineral levels is CRITICAL to your recovery.

The only true way to know where your personal vitamin and mineral levels are is to get tested and work with a qualified professional so you can adjust according to your personal situation. Even while working with a qualified professional, take charge of your own health and cross reference and educate yourself. Use some of the reference websites we provided for you as they'll direct you to new studies and updated information as it comes out.

We all run the risk of being lulled into an imbalanced state simply through our daily habits. Below we'll share some of the most recognized vitamin and mineral imbalances but remember, learning about them and actually having an imbalance are two different things, so don't run out and make dietary changes until you know for sure.

## Calcium

Perhaps the most common and destructive mineral imbalance is excess calcium. This issue has become so important to us we have partnered with Dr. Robert Thompson, author of the book "The Calcium Lie II" (which we give away free), to help get the word out regarding what happens to the body when it has too much calcium.

In short, excess calcium can lead to a whole host of issues including poor digestion, weight gain, thyroid and adrenal malfunction just to name a few. Dr. Thompson gets to the heart of the matter with one statement from his book, "Calcium hardens concrete– Minerals (plural) harden bones."

Due to the harms of excess calcium and the likelihood of causing an excess imbalance when using calcium supplements, we never support the use of supplemental calcium. However, there are natural products that have naturally accruing calcium which is fine. Today, calcium is in almost everything so high dose supplementation is simply not warranted. As a result, you should reconsider taking any product that includes over 100mg of calcium. If you take multiple supplements, please review your diet and all the supplements you take or plan to take.

## Magnesium

Magnesium research supports the fact that most people are deficient in adequate daily intake. Some say magnesium is an "antidote" to excess calcium. It's also critical for hundreds of biochemical reactions throughout the body. Our good friend, Dr. Carolyn Dean, MD, ND wrote a great book titled "The Magnesium Miracle" detailing 22 conditions that stem from a magnesium deficiency. Unfortunately, we do not give that book away but you can find it at Amazon.com or your local book retailer.

## Other Minerals

While calcium and magnesium are the most common mineral imbalances with significant side effects, several others also are frequently in an imbalanced state. Rounding out the list of most common imbalanced minerals are phosphorus, zinc, iron, potassium and selenium.

## Vitamins

There are a few considerations for correcting imbalances within your vitamin intake. First is the fact there are two types of vitamins: fat soluble and water soluble.

Fat soluble vitamins such as vitamins A, D, E and K require fat to be absorbed and stored in your body. If you take a supplement due to an insufficiency in one or more fat soluble vitamins, take it along with the fattest meal of the day for optimal absorption. Be careful with fat soluble vitamin supplements as these vitamins are capable of being stored in excess.

Water soluble vitamins such as vitamin C and the vitamin B family are either used or excreted through urine. Provided you drink adequate water there is little risk of excess buildup though you should still monitor your vitamin levels with testing to see if you require a supplement.

When planning your meals, consider eating smaller portions multiple times per day of both fruits and vegetable. This is a simple way to give your body a continuous source of nutrients it needs. Remember, vitamins are organic in nature and their chemical structure can change with air, heat and pH levels, which means if you cook a vegetable, the vitamins in that vegetable may be affected and not provide you with the optimal nutrient value you need so eat raw vegetables as often as you can.

Finally, there is one simple "rule" regarding the best type of vitamin supplement It should be sourced from plants. The catch term is called a "Whole Food Vitamin," which means it has the whole vitamin, and not a processed chemical substructure (e.g. whole food vitamin C as opposed to ascorbic acid).

## Bottom Line on Vitamin and Mineral Supplements

If you are going to take a mineral supplement, one of your best options is a full spectrum, marine sourced, trace mineral supplement as either evaporated sea water or red marine algae (Lithothamnion calcareum). When looking for a product make sure the version you are considering is low sodium and higher in magnesium.

Vitamin supplements should be whole food based. When taking a supplement for a specific deficiency, take one with minimal additional ingredients so you do not put yourself into excess in another area.

## 5. Imbalance in Gut Microbial Flora

Few think about gut microbial flora imbalances as a health concern when dealing with an acute or chronic inflammatory condition, but flora imbalance in the gut can have far reaching effects on the body. These include constipation, excessive gas, vitamin B deficiencies, hormonal issues, anemia, change in cholesterol levels, skin conditions, trouble managing stress, joint pain, headache, depression, chronic fatigue and making autoimmune diseases harder to manage.

This kind of imbalance, called dysbacteriosis, frequently occurs from improper use or overuse of antibiotics, followed by the consumption of toxins of any type (pesticides, herbicides or even NSAIDs). Eating too much sugar or unhealthy oils can also upset your gut flora. Ask your physician to run a "Dysbiosis Profile" test to determine the current state of your gut flora. Consider making this test part of your annual physical.

Some simple steps you can take to support your good gut flora include eating fermented foods like lacto-fermented fruits and vegetables and unpasteurized yogurt, cheese and kefir.

## 6. Sleep Loss and Inflammation

Yes, I know this is a cookbook, so I will keep this short. Food provides the nutrients to heal our bodies, but our bodies only heal when we sleep. Much like you can have an imbalance in nutrition, you can also become sleep deprived which puts you in an impaired state, according to noted sleep researcher, Dr. James Maas.

I have interviewed Dr. Maas on sleep and performance and his information on sleep might just change your life literally overnight. He is the author of four books on sleep. I highly recommend reading "Power Sleep."

If you have trouble sleeping, there are several good options. Dr. Maas' book is a good starting point. There are many natural herbs and even teas that can help you relax. There are many natural sleep supplements available but I suggest you choose one formulated to put you to sleep, keep you asleep and not leave you feeling groggy in the morning. Good ingredients to look for in a natural sleep supplement include melatonin (2-4mg), magnesium (>100mg), valerian root (>100mg), 5-HTP (100mg) as well as lemon balm, hops flower and passion flower. Take at least one hour before bed.

## 7. Sugar Imbalance

Sugar is perhaps the single worst substance we over consume and it is literally killing us. In the meantime, overconsumption of sugar may also be the most likely single biggest reason you are still inflamed and in pain. Mark Hyman, MD, author of "The Blood Sugar Solution," makes a strong case that excess sugar consumption is responsible for the obesity epidemic, heart disease, diabetes, stroke, dementia and cancer.

How can sugar cause so much harm? When you consume excess simple sugars, a cascade of events begin:

- Free radicals are released
- These cause internal cell damage through oxidation
- Cell damage triggers an immune response
- Immune response = Inflammation

What is insidious about this type of inflammation is it continues as long as you continue to eat sugar. However, it is subacute meaning you may or not feel the effects directly but despite the fact it affects your entire body. If you really want your body to heal and get out of pain, you must control your simple sugar intake.

According to the National Institute of Diabetes and Digestive and Kidney Diseases, the percentage of U.S. adults considered overweight or obese is 68.8%. The interesting part of this statistic is the agency calls it an "energy imbalance." Truthfully, it is also a quality of food issue. You do not become obese eating only fruits, vegetables and high quality proteins. You become obese eating simple sugars.

Dr. Stephen Sinatra describes the cascade effect of sugar on heart disease like this: excessive sugar consumption leads to weight gain. Thus over time, weight gain combined with sustained high insulin levels lead to insulin resistance and diabetes– which further increases the risk of heart disease, as well as the risk for stroke and dementia.

The 1931 Nobel Laureate in Medicine, Otto Warburg, PhD, discovered cancer cells act much differently than normal cells in that they use 10 to 12 times the amount of sugar than healthy cells. He noted cancer cells love acidity and sugar is highly acidic. Further, research has shown sugar can suppress your body's immunity, giving cancer a free ride.

Dr. Hyman's book is a great starting point for learning how to better control your sugar intake. One simple strategy you can take immediately is to drink less sugary drinks. Check sugar levels in your favorite drinks as you may be surprised to learn how energy drinks, sports drinks and teas often have high levels of sugar just like sodas. Also, commit to eating less food processed food products that come in a box or a wrapper.

# Appendix D
# Cooking and Anti-inflammatory Food Prep Tips

1. **Remove stress and blocks around cooking healthy foods.**
   - Do food prep the day before, or several hours before you get hungry.
   - Keep your refrigerator and pantry stocked with healthy food so you aren't tempted to 'cheat' when you are too hungry to cook a full meal.
   - Organize your shopping lists and plan your meals.

2. **Use the leftover/compostable ends of your chopped vegetables to make a broth for soup.**
   - Ends of onions, carrots and celery can be frozen and used later to make into a vegetable broth. Place them in water and bring to a boil. Add any herbs, salt or pepper to the broth for a clear, nurturing liquid meal that is both forgiving and flexible. Experiment by adding chicken bouillon or french soup bouillon to your base broth for added flavor. Freeze the broth for later use, or add extra vegetables while you are cooking the broth to eat immediately (such as potatoes, tomatoes, squash, more carrots, onions and celery, etc.).
   - You can even use cheese rinds in your broths.

3. **Cook for company.**
   - Invite a friend over when experimenting with different recipes to inspire and excite you to try something new.
   - Ask a few friends to do a food share where you cook enough for three families and swap with two other families. This way you only cook once, but have three meals to share.
   - Practice a new-to-you recipe by making it for a potluck.

4. **Tips for baking:**
   - The smaller the item, the higher the temperature and shorter the time needed to bake.
   - Leave eggs and butter out overnight or take them out several hours before needed so they are room temperature when you are ready to use them.

5. **Stovetop cooking:**
   - When cooking or boiling over the stove, food will continue to cook after you turn the heat off. Avoid overcooking by turning the heat off a little earlier and letting the food finish cooking itself with its own internal heat.

6. **Chopping tip:**
   - Add a small amount of sea salt and/or coarse ground black pepper to your cutting board when chopping herbs to help the herbs remain still while chopping.

7. **Onions 101:**
   - Refrigerate onions before slicing to help reduce the sting in your eyes often produced while cutting them.
   - If using onions in a dish for raw consumption (such as salsa or a topping), rinse the diced onion under cold running water to eliminate sulfurous gas that can ruin guacamole and salsa.

8. **Pasta:**
   - Add a little oil to the water while boiling the noodles to keep the noodles from sticking to each other. However, be aware the same principle means the sauce will not stick to the pasta as easily, either. Use oil while cooking pasta at your discretion.
   - Put some parmesan cheese on the noodles before adding sauce. This gives the noodles an added stickiness so the sauce has something to stick to when combined.

9. **Cooking vegetables:**
   - To perk up weepy vegetables, place them in a bath of cold water to perk them up, then pat dry before cooking.
   - When blanching, steaming or boiling vegetables, douse them with ice water once done cooking to help them keep a beautiful color.

10. **Cooking poultry:**
    - Separate a whole chicken when roasting: the breast is thicker than the legs and wings so will need to cook longer. If you cook everything at the same time, you will end up with some pieces dryer than others. The secret is to remove the thinner pieces while letting the thicker pieces cook longer.

# Appendix E
# What to Drink

When considering an anti-inflammatory diet this book would be incomplete without addressing drinks. Like food, certain beverages can help while others will impair your healing.

## Inflammation-Causing Drinks

Reduce or avoid these drinks during healing:

- Alcohol
- Caffeine: coffee, some sweet teas
- Sugary drinks: unnatural juices, some sports drinks, sodas
- Dairy: hot chocolate, milk

**Coffee** is one "Special Consideration" drink we know some people feel they cannot do without which is why we included "The Perfect Cup of Coffee" in the Breakfast recipes. But let's be realistic about what you must do to facilitate healing. At least during your acute phase of healing, try to refrain from high end coffee house brews loaded with high sugar, sweetened flavoring and larger than needed portions. Coffee is highly acidic as well as a diuretic which depletes your body of water, not to mention your body has to process all of the added stuff you put into it. If you are going to drink coffee, try experimenting with some healthier options:

- Non-dairy options
- Coconut oil (to your satisfaction)
- Coconut cream (to your satisfaction)
- Coconut milk (to your satisfaction)
- Butter
- Sweeteners

- Honey (to your satisfaction)
- Stevia (to your satisfaction)
- Coconut sugar (to your satisfaction)
- Flavoring
- Vanilla
- Peppermint
- Turmeric
- Salt
- Cinnamon
- Cardamom

## Anti-Inflammatory Drinks

These drinks are helpful in reducing inflammation:

- Water
- With Lemon
- With Lime
- With a little apple cider vinegar
- Electrolyte concentrates
- Electrolyte tablets
- Teas
- Hot or cold
- Sweetened with honey or stevia
- Ginger
- Turmeric
- Sports drinks are not the best option but you can choose unsweetened brands or dilute the drink by ¼ to ½ with water to help balance out the sugars.
- Berries and greens smoothie (water based)

# Author Bios

## Jesse Cannone

Jesse Cannone, CFT, CPRS, MFT is recognized worldwide as an expert on pain, health and fitness and is featured in major television, radio, magazines and newspapers including NBC, Men's Fitness, Woman's World and The Chicago Tribune.

His cutting-edge *Live Pain Free*® print publication with monthly CD interviews and his free *Less Pain, More Life* email newsletter introduce millions from over 100 countries to a better way of living pain free through improvements in mind, body, and diet. Follow his work at: www.losethebackpain.com

## Tiffany Harelik

Tiffany Harelik is an acclaimed writer for people who love cookbooks, tradition, and travel. Her publishing portfolio spans creative work that includes more than a dozen cookbooks filled with cultural histories and heirloom recipes. After writing for numerous magazines and traditional publishers, she founded Spellbound Publishers. She has a Masters degree in health psychology and enjoys finding the magic in cooking and the great outdoors. Follow her work at: www.tiffanyharelik.com